CARVE!

A book about wood, knives and axes
by Hannes Dahlrot and Henrik Francke

Photography by Miki Anagrius

GINGKO PRESS

Foreword 5

PART 1 ✕ TECHNIQUE

Handicraft 10
Steel 14
Sharpening 17
Hands 24
Surface 34
Wood 38

PART 2 ✕ WOOD CARVING

Moa's sense of wood 53
Carving star from another century 61
A carving club on the island 62

PART 3 ✕ PROJECTS

Butter knives and spatulas 68
Spoons, ladles and scoops 76
Guksi cup 86
Espresso cup 93
Forks, chopsticks and salad utensils 95
Shrink boxes 98
Clothes hooks 108
Knobs and bling 111
Bowl and saucer 115
Combs and hair clips 118
Bartender kit 126
Rhythm instruments 135
Figures and folk caricatures 141

A sharp knife
and a piece of wood ...

That's all that is needed to start carving. With the addition of a saw, chopping block, axe and spoon gouge, it's only imagination and skill that limits what can be carved. A piece of wood contains an infinite number of possible objects – it's only a matter of removing what doesn't belong.

Carving offers a simple doorway into the world of handicraft. It also provides a good understanding of how wood works – from fresh to dry, the widely varied character of different woods, the direction of the grain: no one piece of wood is like another. Each carving project begins with an idea of what each piece of wood might be suitable for: Is it rough, twisted and knotty, or straight, soft and smooth?

Being able to work with your hands may seem increasingly superfluous in our everyday lives, but when the knife succeeds in turning a vision into something concrete, amazing things happen. Wood carving can be addictive, but the consequences are only positive (other than perhaps the occasional injured thumb).

Maybe you tried to carve a butter knife or the like back in shop class, but there are some great reasons to sit back down with a carving knife. When you start carving, you are introduced directly to three-dimensional design. Sketching on a piece of paper is one thing, but adding another dimension makes carving a fun, sculptural challenge. You're using your eyes and hands to create symmetry and harmony – using durable material that also ages beautifully.

$\longrightarrow\longrightarrow$

→→→

This book provides you with ideas for a variety of projects using different types of carving techniques. You'll probably find that carving a Swedish shrink box, for example, is wonderfully meditative in its repetitive simplicity, while fitting the bottom onto the box requires more accuracy and patience. The soft form of the ladle emerges from an angular piece of wood and becomes a humble but beautiful meeting of form and function. Learning to carve knobs and handles might feel good – suddenly you can repair things that you might have thrown away otherwise.

In addition to providing an introduction to wood and a review of knife and axe technology, this book contains thirty-one projects – ranging from classics such as kitchen utensils, ladles, coffee cups and hooks, to bartender kits, beard combs, maracas and chopsticks. In addition, there are portraits of some inspiring people who are passionate, in different ways, about the craft of carving wood. This book came into being during a meeting between Hannes and Henrik – the former a qualified and experienced fine-quality carpenter, figure carver and wood crafts-man, and the latter an enthusiastic knife novice. We hope you find that our collaboration has led to an educational and inspirational book.

With a few exceptions, it is Hannes's handwork that is included in the book, but remember, it's not the final result that's important – you will realize this after carving for a while. The real reward is the experience: the smell of the wood as you carve, wood shavings falling to the floor and the changing colors of the wood as you carve.

X

GOOD LUCK!

PART 1 ✕ TECHNIQUE

Handicraft

Fresh and dry wood > The piece of wood you select for carving is called a blank. Although every blank will feel different when you cut into it, the type of tree the wood comes from is less of a factor than how recently the tree was felled or the branch was cut. Wood that is fresh – or green or raw, as it is sometimes called – is much softer than when it has dried. Fresh wood is easy to shape with an axe and the knife cuts through it without much effort.

How long it takes for a blank to dry depends on its size and thickness, and how and where it is stored. If you have a fresh branch or stem, store it outdoors in the shade or in a cool place, where it will dry more slowly than indoors.

Once you start carving and the bark is removed, the blank dries pretty quickly, so it's a good idea to keep carving and finish your basic shape while the wood is still fresh. A roughly carved ladle is usually dry after a week indoors. If you want to take a break from carving, you can put the blank in the fridge or outdoors to keep it fresh a little longer. Some carving projects, such as shrink boxes, require that you finish carving before the wood has dried, as the construction is based on using the shrinkage that occurs when the moisture comes out of the wood. You can wrap the blank in a damp towel, put it in a plastic bag and store it in the fridge to keep it fresh a bit longer – but it will buy you only a few days.

For the best surface finish, with a nice sheen and sharp cuts, allow the fresh blank to dry after the basic shape is carved. You will not get any luster as long as the blank is still moist.

Before you start, make sure the blank is a bit bigger than what you'd like the finished project to be. Shrinkage occurs during drying and wood tends to split as it dries, so if you start with extra you can cut off any cracks at the ends (known as the end grain), if needed.

A few rules of thumb: To reduce the risk of splitting, here are a few rules of thumb. Slow down the drying process by wrapping the blank in a towel and placing it in a box. Also, the bigger the piece of wood you start with, the better you can deal with cracks that might occur when the blank dries. You can avoid the pith in the middle of the wood where most of the cracks usually occur. The thinner and more knot-free your finished, carved product is, the less end grain you'll have, and therefore the less risk of cracks during drying. You can try sealing the end grain with glue or boiled potatoes, but it is sticky and messy and must eventually be carved away. And, unfortunately, if the blank wants to crack somewhere, it usually does – no matter how careful you are with drying.

+ *Carving fresh wood is a joy, but with a sharp knife, carving even dry wood is nothing to complain about. We assert that you can find pleasure in any kind of carving, whether you have cut down a tree on your own property or you've purchased a bag of wood.*

It's much easier to get dry wood than fresh for most of us who don't own forests – we can buy wood at lumber yards, hobby shops and even convenience stores. But don't give up on the idea of carving with fresh wood just because you live in town. Take a walk in the park after a heavy storm (take a small folding saw with you if you can). The urban wood carver is always extra attentive when passing through cemeteries, community garden plots, parks, villages or other places where and trees regularly fall. If you explain that you are looking for wood to carve, nice arborists and gardeners will usually be happy to donate a branch or block for artistic purposes.

Since most of us don't have access to irregular-shaped pieces of wood that might be perfect for carving a ladle, for example, we have based most of this book's projects on straight wood, which is much easier to find.

Steel

The carving knife > It cannot be overstated that the sharpness of the knife is the most important thing of all. To carve with a dull knife is like backing up a hill with skis on. It quite simply takes away all the fun of something that should be a real pleasure, so always be diligent in sharpening your tools.

Having a handsome hand-forged knife is great, but it is not a necessity. For approximately $25 or $30, you can buy a well-crafted factory-made carving knife. A suitable knife has a relatively short blade with a small "belly." Some knives have a crossguard that sticks out at the base of the blade – the cross guard protects, but only when chopping, and it makes the knife awkward to carve with.

TO CONSIDER!

Bark can contain gravel and dirt which quickly makes the edge become dull and ragged. If you have a knife that needs to be sharpened or one that you are not so particular about, you can carve away the bark with that one instead of sacrificing your freshly sharpened steel.

Use the blade's sheath or case and make sure the knife does not slide around in a kitchen drawer. Cooking with your carving knife is also not recommended; there is a risk that the edge will dull.

Some carving knives have a blunt tip and others are pointed. Points can break off but also help with the small details. A wide or large-bellied blade does not work as well as a narrow or smaller-bellied one if you are going to hollow out a piece of wood; for example, when you make shrink boxes.

If you want just one knife, usually a 5 cm blade is fine. For children, there are special knives with handles for smaller hands.

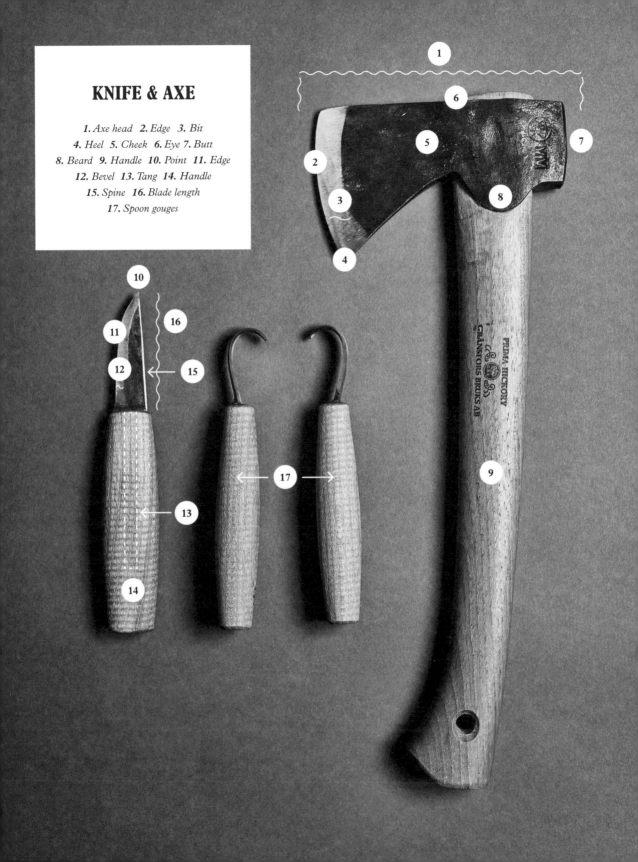

KNIFE & AXE

1. Axe head 2. Edge 3. Bit
4. Heel 5. Cheek 6. Eye 7. Butt
8. Beard 9. Handle 10. Point 11. Edge
12. Bevel 13. Tang 14. Handle
15. Spine 16. Blade length
17. Spoon gouges

Spoon gouges > Spoon gouges (or crooked knives, as they are also called), with their curved blades, are used to gouge out the wood. The size of the curve on the knife dictates how deep down you can gouge. With a large and flat bend you will not go down too deep. Hand-forged spoon gouges are preferred since the factory-made ones often have blades that are so angled that the turning radius isn't very good. Avoid factory-made spoon gouges with sharpened edges on both sides of the blade – it makes it impossible to handle the knife blade with your fingers. Instead of a two-bladed knife, we recommend having two knives with edges on different sides, that is, a right knife and a left knife.

THINK ABOUT…

… being particularly careful when sharpening spoon gouges because they are more difficult to sharpen than straight knives.

An alternative to two spoon gouges is a regular gouge, which looks like a chisel with a rounded edge. With a regular gouge, you do not have to think about which of the right or left spoon gouges are appropriate in any direction, and the technique for gouging out comes quite naturally. Many like to secure the blank to a workbench when using the gouge. Then you can use both hands, and it reduces the risk of slipping. In the end, it's up to personal taste if you want to hollow out with a spoon gouge or a regular gouge.

Axe > The axe is one of humankind's oldest known tools and is available in a variety of forms and designs. For woodworking, there is everything from neat little carving axes to solid, heavy, broad axes for house building. There are axes, known as adzes, which have an edge that's perpendicular to the handle. The adze is used as a chisel, and the gutter adze, with an inwardly curved head and a bowl-shaped edge, is used for hollowing out. The carving axe, which is most interesting to us as wood carvers, requires control and therefore has a shorter shaft and less weight than a splitting axe. The head may have a recess so that the fingers of the hand can support the head itself. The blade usually tends to be slightly bent to get the cutting motion you want when you carve with the axe. The safer you feel with the axe, the farther out on the handle you can hold and the more power you have, but the precision cuts are more difficult. Think about how you stand when you swing the axe – if you are unlucky and hit wrong, the axe may bounce off the wood and change course. Be sure to keep your chopping block clean from dirt, sand and pebbles, otherwise the edge on your axe will be quickly damaged.

Sharpening

It takes a lot to make a knife work well. The angle of the edge must not be too flat, otherwise it won't penetrate the wood. The angle must also not be too steep or the knife will wedge into the cut between the wood and the chip. An angle of about 23–27 degrees is best. The quality of the steel is also important if the knife is to stay sharp for a long time. The hardness of the steel must be just right; if a knife is made of steel that is too hard, the edge can be broken off, and if the steel is too soft, the blade can bend.

Honing the knife > It's an absolute must to sharpen your knives, because carving with a dull knife is not worth the effort. To maintain and take care of your knives, you need two knife sharpeners. They are available in several grain sizes, and you will need both a coarse (1,000 grain) and a fine (8,000 grain) sharpener to get a good sharp knife. Sharpening stones come in two categories: water and oil. To sharpen using sandstone and other absorbent stones, you use water to soak the stones first, and for Arkansas stones and other less absorbent stones, you soak them in oil. We recommend using water sharpening stones, which is the easiest method.

Some knife edges are conically shaped. The rounded edges allow you to even sharpen the inside of the rounded edges.

Soak the honing stones for a while before you sharpen your knives on them. Always work at the same angle as the blade was initially ground and start with the coarse-grained sharpener. Hold the knife with the edge toward you and push the bevel of the blade against the stone with your thumb. Pull the knife back and forth over the sharpener or around in small circles. Occasionally rinse off the honing stone so that it does not dry out. It does not need to be under running water, as in the picture, in order to work. When grinding the other side, hold the knife in the correct position with your forefinger instead. Switch back and forth between sides a couple of times before switching to the fine-grained sharpener and repeat the procedure. Both sides should be sharpened equally.

Strop › A strop is a leather strap that you put a sharpening paste on and then draw the knife's edge against it to further hone the steel. Some like to have the strop mounted onto a hard surface. Others sharpen directly on a flat wooden piece with sharpening paste. Many wet sharpening machines, or wet grinders, are equipped with a motor-driven strop.

In the picture, Hannes uses the back of his belt, otherwise free-hanging strops made of cowhide are the most common. One end of the strop is fitted with a hook so you can hang up the strop while sharpening, and at the other end there is a handle you can use to stretch it out. When using a free-hanging strop, it is important that it does not give way when you're working against it. If the strop is soft, it can round the edge of the knife instead of sharpening it. The edge can also be rounded if you press the steel too hard against the strop so that the leather bends around the edge. Use sharpening paste that's made for fine honing, with a grain size of around 0.003 mm.

Put a thin bead of paste on the strop. Lay the bevel of the knife on top of the paste and pull a few times on each side of the knife. Try to be light-handed when you hone and hold the knife straight out from the strop. Always sharpen with the edge; if you sharpen toward the edge you will sooner or later cut into the leather and damage it.

Grindstone › After a period of carving, your knife, no matter how much you take care of it, will need a machine sharpening. The edge will deteriorate and receive damage that cannot be honed away. A grindstone gives the knife a convex beveled edge that can be sharpened a couple of times before you have to sharpen it on the grindstone again.

Sharpening and honing your tools is an important part of the handicraft and, at the very least, it is very satisfying to make a dull, useless knife razor-sharp again. If you become a carving enthusiast, sooner or later you will end up wishing you could invest a couple hundred dollars on your own wet sharpening machine.

TOOLS

You will go a long way with just axes and knives, but sometimes there are situations where a few more tools could come in handy. Here are some of our favorites.

1. A Japanese saw, or pull saw, is one that is pulled toward you, unlike most other saws. Because the blade does not have to withstand pressure, it can be made thin. It is usually stated in the number of teeth per 30 mm how finely toothed the saw is. The smaller saw in the picture has 36 teeth/30 mm and the blade is 0.2 mm thick. The other has 26/30 mm and the blade is 0.76 mm thick. Used mostly for dry wood.

2. Pruning saws are used by arborists, gardeners, wood carpenters and others who saw fresh wood. The saw blades are specially sharpened with multiple angles, which gives a smoother cut than conventional saws. The saw also cuts on the draw, making it easier to use.

3. A coping saw is used for cutting irregular lines and shapes. The thin blade can be threaded through a drilled hole and is therefore practical to use when doing relief carving. The saw blade should be clamped securely so that the teeth dig in when the saw is pushed away from you.

4. A clamp is used for holding the wood securely or for compressing two pieces of wood during gluing. Clamps are available in a variety of sizes, depths and designs. With the screw clamp, the wood is secured by tightening the handle until the clamp is locked between the upper jaw and the plate at the end of the screw. A one-handed clamp or quickturn clamp is tightened by pumping the handle. As the name suggests, it can be tightened and loosened with one hand.

5. A gouge or chisel is used for hollowing out bowls or working on curved wooden surfaces. The edge is U-shaped and is available in a variety of sizes and radiuses. For carving out deep hollows, there are curved gouges. When working with gouges, it is best if you can clamp the piece of wood you are working on in place so you can cut with a lot more power. The angle of the bevel is usually approximately 25 degrees, but can be adapted to the wood you are working on. For hard wood, a larger angle is suitable and for soft wood, a smaller one.

6. A wooden mallet can be made in one or two pieces. If you make your own wooden mallet, you should use a really gnarly wood. If it's twisted or burly, it is harder and holds up better against bangs and blows, and there's less chance of the mallet breaking.

7. Sanding cloth or sandpaper is used mainly in the removal of irregularities in the wood. In the past natural minerals were used, such as quartz, flint and emery, so the term sandpaper was more correct than it is now. Today aluminum oxide, a synthetic abrasive, is most commonly used. The number on the back of the sandpaper indicates the coarseness of the grit; the higher the number, the finer the grit.

A sanding cloth has a significantly longer life and is better suited for grinding uneven surfaces than sandpaper, which falls apart quickly when sanding a surface that is not flat. If the sanding cloth gets clogged with shavings, rinse it with water and most of the shavings will usually disappear. Avoid carving on a sanded surface since sandpaper releases its grain, which sits in the wood and dulls the edge of the knife when cutting into it. The sandpaper in the picture is 30 cm in diameter, has 120 grains and is for a disc sander.

8. Two-part epoxy consists of a base and a hardener stored in two containers and mixed together in the desired amount before application. Two-part epoxy usually does not need air to cure as it is a chemical reaction between the substances that makes the glue harden. Two-part epoxy is usually water resistant and does not shrink when it hardens. Avoid getting the adhesive glue on your skin.

9. A drill bit designed for wood (such as the egg cup drill bit shown in the photo) can be fitted into a drill to use as a rotary cutting tool. Drills are available in a variety of designs tailored for different purposes. The spiral drill bit is the most common model for wood. It has two edges that go all the way along the spiral. The main task of the spiral is to remove the shavings. The center drill bit, with a sharp tip and two radial cutting edges that bore into wood, is a good choice if you want to drill a larger hole with a hand drill. Since the center drill bit has no spiral to clean out the shavings from the hole, you have to remove the drill and do it yourself. An egg cup drill bit makes a hole with a round bottom.

10. Talmeter is a measuring tape used to measure internal and external dimensions as well as cylinder diameters. The measuring tape is pulled out by hand, but is automatically retracted when the button is pressed. Dimensions are given in millimeters, the red digits you read when you flip the tape over. At the end of the handle there is a marking edge that is used to make markings in the wood. There is a small hole in the tape where a nail can be used to mark the wood. The name Talmeter originated from the initials of the inventor, Ture Anders Ljungberg. If you pull the tape all the way out the year in which it is manufactured is printed there, and whoever has the oldest one wins (they stopped being manufactured in 2005).

A mortise chisel (not pictured) has a straight edge and is used to work and cut loose pieces of wood. Some shafts are reinforced with a metal ring at the end to withstand the impact of a wooden mallet. The angle of the edge is the same as for gouges.

Hands

Always start by looking at the intended wood for the project. Is it straight or bent? Is it twisted along its axis? Are there any knots and, if so, where do they sit in relation to your envisioned form? A common beginner's mistake is to pick up a piece of wood and start carving only to realize, after some time of enthusiastic work, that this particular block was far from ideal. It is no fun to carve for an hour or so and then to realize that the wood does not have the strength that is needed at a particular point because of a knot, for example.

If you begin with a smaller branch or stick, there may be no need to split it – in that case, you can just get started carving. However, be aware that the risk of splitting during drying is greater when you do not first cleave away the central pith of the wood. If you have a larger branch, or a block from a tree trunk, start by splitting up your wood for your blank.

To avoid bandages › Avoiding injury is about being safety conscious at all times. Think constantly about where you have your hands, fingers and legs, and visualize in advance where the axe will end up if it slips or if the chopping block tips over. Concentrate on the task and do not rush. Make sure that children and pets will not disturb you.

What to consider when carving with a knife: Most of the time you cut yourself when changing your grip or when putting down the knife – it's easy to lose focus a few seconds too early. When you carve toward yourself, be sure to use a grip that allows knife strokes with a clear stop. If you are worried about cutting yourself, you can buy Kevlar gloves such as glaziers use; they protect quite well against getting cut. The disadvantage is that, if you get used to them, you feel naked carving without them.

☺ *How old a child should be to start carving we leave up to parents to decide. Keep in mind that commotion and running around do not go together with sharp tools. Since children love to be involved and want to carve but lack the age and maturity, a piece of bark and a potato peeler can be used instead. It is still possible to get cut, but it will not be fatal. And a bark boat is certainly nothing to complain about.*

Cleave › For cleaving wood, there are special cleavers, but it is also works to use an axe. The best control is achieved by tapping the axe with a sturdy wooden mallet a tool that is easy to make yourself with the help of the axe. Make the head of the mallet with a hard wood, for instance elm or some type of fruit tree, so that it does not break when you use it

to hit axes and wedges. The advantage of making the mallet head with gnarly and hard wood is it is more durable. Avoid metal to metal and do not hit the axe's neck with a hammer or similar tool. The risk is that the axe will be deformed, or that the eye gets pulled out and the handle comes loose.

To form a base for the cleaving, the best and safest is a sturdy chopping block. It is easy to slip with the axe, so you should be sure in advance that the

axe cannot miss the block and hit your leg instead. Set what you are going to split in the middle of the block so that the axe head will safely end up in the block. Stand with one leg a bit behind the other, as far away from the axe's possible pendulum movement as you can stand without losing your balance. It's good if the chopping surface is not completely smooth; having bumps and grooves can help keep the subject in place when working with it. Cleave out

your blank along the wood's grain direction, since cleaving in any other way is not possible. If instead, you were to saw a slice off a trunk in the same way as cutting a loaf of bread, the wood would be sure to split when it dries, because basically the whole surface is made up of end grain.

If you want to be extra careful, determine exactly where the wood piece is going to split, otherwise go by feel. If you're going to split a smaller piece, it is smart to cut off the bark on both sides where the blank will split. Then you will see clearly whether it splits exactly as you intended. If it's a crooked blank, you may need to insert a wedge or move the axe along the crack in the wood to complete the split.

with a thicker stem, first cleave it in the middle and then split it up depending where you want the rings to be. For example, for a butter knife project it is best to have the rings in the blade.

Try to read the piece of wood before cleaving: Where are the knots and how will they affect your ready-cut "fillet"? When cleaving a thicker trunk for carving, it is usually done through the pith or core. It is from the pith that the wood tends to split, so cleaving it in the middle and then cutting away the pith reduces the risk of cracks later. If you're working

The direction of the grain in your blank will determine how you will later carve it and how durable your finished product will be.

A good way to start is to cleave out a rectangular blank with rather flat sides. You can then easily figure out the shape you want. If you do not have access to an axe, you can cleave thin objects using a knife along with a wooden or rubber mallet.

Roughly cut and carve ›You now have a rectangular blank, and it is time to draw out the contours of what you want to carve with a pencil. Check whether you can cleave off more material if you make a stop cut with a saw, that is, a cut that stops the cleaving at a certain point. It is also possible to cut this kind of stop directly with the ax. Just make sure you do not cut your hand that is holding the wood. It may be helpful to use a chopping block that has a recess to lean the piece against if you want to cut a stop. You can also put the blank on the chopping block and chop down until you get a deep enough notch.

Cut out the rough shape with the axe. It is safest to cut toward the lines by removing a little bit of the material at a time. A good technique is to chop a little ways into the wood until the axe has wedged fast. Then tap your axe and the blank as one unit down onto the chopping block until the chip has loosened and the axe is free. Similarly, you can start a cut by placing the axe edge against the place on the wood where you want the cut to start and then hit the axe and the blank into the block. If you want to chop off a thin chip, it may be best to put the blank on the chopping block and split it from above using the wooden mallet.

Cut out the rough shape with the axe. The safer you feel with the axe, the more wood you can remove. It's usually worth doing as much as possible with the axe because it goes more quickly, and you also save the sharpness of the knife for the more detailed work.

Now, it's time to switch over to the knife. Start by sitting down. A bench or a chair without armrests works best. Sitting at the kitchen table is also good for most carving techniques.

Carving is about cutting wood. This means that the knife's edge will move over the wood, so that it really becomes a cut along the edge of the knife. The principle is always to carve with the direction of the wood's grain and not against it. You will quickly find that sometimes the knife cuts smoothly and with fine shavings, and sometimes the wood breaks where you carve instead of slicing off – that's when you carve in the wrong direction related to the grain of the wood, and you have to change directions either by turning the wood or by changing your grip. Keep in mind that as soon as the wood starts to flake off, it means you are probably carving in the wrong direction.

In most cases, the force must come from the hand, not from the arm. If you think of a typical child carving, you will notice how he or she carves with their whole arm, and that the knife at the end of the cut goes up into the air in a fairly uncontrolled way. Avoid this.

The goal is to carve powerfully but slowly. It's a controlled, powerful motion, but moving only a short distance on the blank. Sometimes the wood is moved against the knife rather than the knife moving over the wood.

When you start carving with a knife, it is often a good idea to continue to use a blank that has four distinct sides. If you begin to round the edges too early, it is easy to lose the shape. Begin with the top side, then go over to the edges. As long as you have not begun rounding the edges, it's easy to re-draw the shape if you need to. Finish cutting a line, bevel, or side from top to bottom before moving on to the next detail. In other words, move forward systematically, not a little here and a little there. Take breaks and look at the wood from different angles, feel it with your fingers to get an idea of its thickness, shape, and symmetry. Trust your eye: If it is looking good, then it is working.

If it does not look symmetrical but it's hard to discern what's wrong, here's a simple trick that works if you have not rounded the edges: Place the item on a piece of paper and trace the shape with a pen. If the object leans, it usually works to first put the paper and then the blank against your thigh and draw around it. It is important that the paper is positioned right up against the blank so the sketch is accurate. Cut the paper along the lines and fold it right down the middle. Now you will clearly see what is causing the sides to be asymmetrical. Cut away what is uneven – often you have to take away a little on both sides. Place the paper onto the blank, trace around the blank and carve according to the lines.

Another way to carve is to ignore the sketch and the desire to keep the blank's edges as long as possible. Let your mind and purpose with the carving determine your approach. Sometimes it's wonderful to "free carve" and just let the shape become what it wants to.

Carving grip > There are a lot of different grips and techniques you can use when carving – what one prefers is different from person to person. After a while you will discover your favorites, and you'll only use other grips if nothing else works. Some grips are suitable for fresh, easily carved wood but do not work as well with dry wood. Sometimes you use the tip of the knife and sometimes the part closest to the handle.

Since it is primarily the wrists and hands that do the work when carving, the size and strength of your hands can play a part in the grip you prefer. The arms are usually held in close to the body so that carving becomes less sweeping and more controlled. Some rest their elbows against their knees when they carve, which also works well. The main thing is that the hands are supported by the body so that they can focus on the knife and the piece of wood.

When you first start carving, there's a lot to keep track of, and you can expect that it will take some time and practice before your hands work effectively. The knife hand should learn what angle the edge should have against the wood. The other hand, will learn how to hold the blank and move against the knife at the same time. And then you'll understand when to use each grip – and learn how to carve slowly but with power. Later you will learn to interpret the information about the wood that the knife blade sends you.

Once you get into carving, the grip comes naturally, and you rarely get hurt. But before you get there, keep in mind where you position the hand that's holding the blank. That's the hand in the danger zone if you should slip with the knife.

Carving forward is the image of carving most people have, but this is not a very useful grip. You may have a lot of power, but it is difficult to control it safely. The hand and knife fly uncontrollably forward as the chips drop from the piece of wood. It can work well for rough working of fresh wood so you have long fine chips, but in dry wood it is rarely used. A safer way is to carve forward a little until the knife grips the wood, then continue the cut by pulling the hand that holds the wood against the knife. This makes it impossible for the knife to fly away, and the carving becomes more controlled. If you like this technique, you can also get support with your knife hand in front of your knee.

→→

Some carvers make use of **the scissors grip,** in which the knife and blank are held up against the chest, with your elbows toward your body so that the force comes from your back muscles. This method may be worth trying if you do not get enough power from any other.

By pushing **with the thumb,** you can carve forward with both power and control. With your knife hand, make sure the blade is at a right angle to the wood while pushing the back of the knife with the hand holding the blank.

Carving artist Döderhultaren was very fond of **carving toward himself,** so much so that he finally made a hole in his work coat at chest height. Hold the end of the blank and press it slightly against your stomach or chest. Carve with the knife toward you but angle it so that the tip is away from you. Hold your arms into your body so that you can carve slowly but with power. If you like, you can push the knife back with the hand that is holding the blank, like playing the violin.

Carving against the thumb is a good technique, especially when you're going to bevel off an edge or carve to the end of a shaft. Place the thumb of your knife hand against the back of the knife and carve by closing your hand and pushing away with your thumb. Try to place the thumb of your knife's hand so that it is protected behind the piece of wood you carve on so that you do not cut yourself. With the other hand, hold on to the blank.

If you do not have an edge to brace your thumb against, you can *press the thumb of your knife hand against the blank with the hand that is holding the wooden piece.* Another option is to *hold the knife blade against the blank with your index finger.*

Spoon gouge or crooked knife. With the spoon gouge, you usually switch between carving toward and away from yourself. For example, if you're carving the handle of a ladle, hold the handle and carve with the right spoon gouge on the right side by carving away from yourself, and *push with your thumb.* Then turn the ladle so that you're holding the ladle's bowl, and carve the other side of the ladle by *carving toward your thumb* with the left spoon gouge.

Push with your thumb.

Carve against yourself.

Carve against the thumb.

Press in the thumb of your knife hand.

Hold down the knife blade with your forefinger.

Push with the thumb (spoon gouge).

Surface

Sanding is not not ideal. After using coarse sandpaper, you have many steps in front of you in order to get as smooth a result as when it is cut. And by then you are covered with dust and bored, having created something that looks machine-made. With a really sharp knife and a dry blank, you get the finest surface and gloss.

In Sweden, carved figures are often painted and stained, but we like to keep the natural color of wood for everyday items.

If you want, you can oil your carved items for a hardier and more durable surface. Which oil is suitable depends on the application. For a spoon that you will eat with, you want to use a natural and harmless oil that tempers. A tempering oil gives a hard, resinous texture when exposed to air for a long time, which makes the wood harder and more resistant. There are only a handful of oils that have this property. In addition to linseed oil and tung oil, as discussed below, poppy seed oil, walnut oil and oil extracted from seeds of *Perilla frutescens* (in the mint family) are the most common.

Oils that do not cure get absorbed into the wood and make it greasy. It gives the objects a certain protection against moisture, but if you are unlucky, the oil can get rancid or even mildewed, so it is best to avoid common cooking oils.

Wax lays like a film on cut surfaces and does not penetrate into the wood but works well on a sanded surface.

Keep in mind that oil-soaked rags and paper can spontaneously combust in exceptional conditions, so do not forget to rinse them or clean up the traces immediately after you are finished, or store the rags in a container with a sealed lid if you plan to use them more than once.

Linseed oil > Linseed oil is made from the seeds of the flax plant. To extract high-quality oil, there are many factors that need to be considered: seed type, planting, sunshine, soil, harvest time, and, last but not least, the methods used to extract the oil and process it. With all of that in mind, you can see that linseed oil is a complex product, and that's why the time it takes to cure linseed oil varies a lot; some will cure in twelve hours, others in four weeks, most of them somewhere in between. Linseed oil does not dry but rather it cures through oxidation. This means that oxygen binds to the oil and forms a new heavier molecule – therefore, it is important to have a good oxygen supply and heat when you want a good and quick result.

There are different methods for extracting the oil from the seed. Cold pressing is the most common and provides a high-quality oil with little residue, unlike oil extracted by heat pressing or extraction.

Cold pressed raw linseed oil is derived from letting the oil be after pressing. It has slightly smaller molecules and penetrates deeper into the wood, but, on the other hand, it contains proteins, antioxidants and mucilage that can act as a breeding ground for both mold and fungus. Kitchenware treated with raw linseed oil can have a taste for a long time. It may take months before the oil has penetrated, as oxygen does not enter the wood piece and oxidize the oil. The advantage is that it is guaranteed to be free from additives, which many appreciate. If the oil has a greenish hue, the seeds have been pressed too early and it is not suitable for surface treatment.

Cold-pressed boiled linseed oil is heated to 150–250 degrees Celsius for a long time, which causes a large portion of the residues in it to be destroyed or separated from the oil. The oil begins to oxidize and creates larger molecules that more easily form a surface. Boiled linseed oil is ideal for surface treatment, and it can also be used as a binding agent for linseed oil paint. If you are eager to use linseed oil, we think that cold-pressed boiled linseed oil is a wise choice. Look for a light oil without sediment on the bottom. You can make the oil lighter by bleaching it in sunlight, for example in a glass jar on a window sill, or outside on the balcony.

Procedure > Brush the piece of wood generously with oil and let it absorb the oil for at least one hour. Every now and then, brush with a small amount of oil, let the wood piece absorb it and wipe away any excess oil with a rag. If you do not remove the excess, the oil will solidify and lay like a film on the object. Kitchen utensils and other items that will be in contact with moisture can be left in a can of linseed oil to absorb it for a couple of hours. Wipe off the excess oil and let it dry. If you want the item to cure quickly, make sure it has warmth and good access to air. It is common to thin linseed oil with chemicals like turpentine and naphtha for a faster cure, but it just adds a thinner layer so you get only a slightly faster result. We recommend using only natural linseed oil. If you want better penetration and thinner oil, you can warm it up to about 50 degrees Celsius then treat the wood with warm oil.

Paraffin oil › Paraffin oil is a scent-free and taste-free mineral oil that is often used for surface treatment of kitchen benches and cutting boards, so it works well for the craftsman's needs when it comes to making items that will be used with food. It does not cure, it only makes the wood greasy and hence more water resistant.

Danish oil › For projects that will not be used in cooking or eating, Danish oil is a favorite. It cures quickly and penetrates deep. Danish oil is a mixture of tung oil, resins and other vegetable oils that penetrate the wood and protect it against moisture and rot. It does not lay as a film on the wood as wax and lacquer do; instead, the surface remains virtually unchanged. The shade of the wood deepens slightly when it has been oiled, but it retains almost the same color as it had before. Apply the oil with a brush or cloth, let it soak in for a few minutes, then wipe off what the wood has not absorbed. After six hours, the oil has cured, and you can add another layer of oil. Rags used to apply or wipe off excess oil can, in certain conditions, spontaneously combust, so allow them to dry in a safe place or rinse them with water.

Tung oil › Tung oil is extracted by pressing seeds from the Chinese tung tree, *Vernicia fordii*. It is a curing oil that hardens when exposed to air. Tung oil does not noticeably darken with age, unlike many other oils, and is claimed to be less sensitive to mold than, for example, linseed oil. The whole tung tree is poisonous, which also applies to the fruits and seeds of the tree, and thus the oil extracted from them. Because of the toxicity of tung oil, it is therefore wiser to use linseed oil on items that will be close to food.

Wood

Everything begins with trees. Tall, short, crooked or slender. It is difficult to find a more powerful sight than an iconic sheltering tree looking down over a court-yard and following the lives of people generation after generation. The annual rings in a full-grown tree testify to how a tree in the forest fought for its place and, through each season, gained more and more authority in its environment.

Ground water is sucked up through the roots of the tree and surface water is transported through the taproot. Inside the outer wood is the heartwood, and right in the center of the tree is the often slightly porous pith. When photosyn-thesis performs its magic in the leaves (converting water and carbon dioxide into carbohydrates through sunlight), sap – the tree's nutrition – forms and is transported throughout the tree via the inner bark. From the inner bark to the core of the tree are medullary rays that divide up the nutrients in the wood. These rays are found in all trees but are only visible in some. Look at the piece of oak shown on page 46, for example, where the rays are clearly visible.

There is an obvious division in the forest between deciduous and coniferous trees, but it's also interesting to note the difference between ring-porous and dif-fuse-porous trees. To do that we have to look closer than just leaves and needles, through the annual rings all the way into the cell structure. An annual ring is cre-ated during a season: The first half of the growing season gives spring wood and the other half gives summer wood. The spring wood on ring-porous deciduous trees like oak, elm and ash consists of large cells, unlike the summer wood, which consists of smaller cells. Ring-porous trees have layers of large vessels or pores in spring wood and smaller vessels in summer wood, which causes the density of the wood to become uneven. Practically, this means that the carver should avoid these woods for projects with fine-cut details – for example, the combs on page 118. The proportion of spring wood versus summer wood in conifers also plays a major role – tight annual rings mean a smaller proportion of spring wood with low density, and thus results in a stronger piece.

HERE FOLLOWS...

... a selection of trees that the enthusiastic carver may encounter. And a little reminder: Unless you have express permission, do not saw down a tree or cut branches that are not your own. Not even for carving purposes.

Alder. Alder is the only one of the leafy trees that produces seed cones. There are two variants: gray alder and common or sticky alder. As its alternate name suggests, the common alder's leaves, buds and shoots are sticky. Alders grow well with water, and the wood is thus resistant to moisture. As a carving material, it is a classic, certainly owing a lot to Swedish master wood carver Döderhultaren for having carved all his works in alder. In addition to figure carving, alder is the number one material for wooden shoes.

Elm. Elm tolerates the cold better than other noble leafy trees, and therefore is also more widespread in the north. Unfortunately, the population of elms in their habitats have been severely affected by elm disease, a contagious disease caused by a fungus. The ring-porous wood is heavy and hard, and the fibers are often twisted. A strong grip and stubbornness are therefore advisable when carving in elm. It has been traditionally used for mill wheels and boat keels because of its durability.

Ash. Ash is strong and tough, and is therefore used for everything from axe handles to parquet floors. It's relatively hard to carve with, so make sure your knife is sharp. The wider the annual rings the stronger the wood, but also the harder it is to work with. The trees can be impressively tall but, just like the elm is often faced with a fatal disease, so is the ash, in this case, ash tree disease. Sometimes the ash is called the King tree because the leaves arrive last and leave first. It is also known in ancient Norse myths as Yggdrasil, the world tree covering the entire sky.

Aspen. The saying "trembling like an aspen leaf" is not plucked out of thin air; the aspen is easily recognizable for its rounded leaves with wavy edges and long leaf stems that whisper with the slightest breeze. Aspen is not generally valued, as it grows like a weed – but as carving material, it is quite nice, with fine white wood that's easy to carve. Slim aspens are nice to make shrink boxes from.

TREE TYPES

1. Apple
2. Beech
3. Hazel
4. Elm
5. Cherry
6. Laburnum
7. Birch
8. Oak
9. Aspen

Birch. The birch is easy to romanticize, with its white bark and nostalgic aura. And with good reason, because as a carving material, birch is perfect. The birch is a common leafy tree, and its wood is soft but at the same time sturdy. In birch, it is possible to create intricate patterns without the risk of losing any detail.

There are many different species of birch, the most common being white birch and silver birch but, when buying wood, they usually lump them together as the same tree. The bark of white birch is smooth and does not have the thick bark that silver birch has. Wooden measuring sticks are made almost exclusively of white birch, which is easier to work with than spring birch. Curly birch, with its extremely crusty bark and with its intricate color changes, makes craftsmen very excited. Knobby growths on silver birch are called burls, and even they hide amazing textures.

As good as the birch is to carve in, it's poor at withstanding rain and nasty weather, so if you're doing something for outdoor use, a treatment to avoid rot is recommended. The same applies if you fell a birch – with roots left on, the tree rots quickly if left lying on the ground.

Beech. The beautiful contiguous beech forests found in southern Sweden have their very own character. Where the beech has grown in peace, it can reach great heights – the tallest tree measured in Sweden was a (now storm-wrecked) beech in Skåne that, in the 1950's, measured an impressive 44 meters high.

Beech wood is even and hard, and it is common in furniture because it is available in large, knot-free lengths. Ice cream sticks are made of beech for the simple reason that the wood has no taste or smell. If you fail at a craft project made with beech, it can be comforting to know that beech wood makes good charcoal.

Oak. The oak is one of the thickest trees, having documented specimens with trunks of up to 13 meters in circumference. The reason that the oak has become such an esteemed tree is its suitability for shipbuilding. At its heyday, the oak was protected in Sweden and could only be used with the king's approval.

Oak may sound fancy, but for carving it's a super hard material, at least for beginners. But just because it is hard does not mean that it's durable – ring porosity makes oak pretty fragile. In oak wood, you can clearly see the medullary rays.

Juniper. This is one of the world's most widespread coniferous tree. Juniper often looks like a bush, but can in some places grow to 15 meters high. Juniper is often considered best for carving. And, of course it is a classic butter knife material – but for a beginner, it can be quite discouraging if the blank is crooked and knotty. As you progress with carving, however, it can be nice to carve with juniper, with its beautiful rings and wonderful smell. Traditionally, it is not only butter knives that have been made of juniper, but also other charming tableware, such as butter tubs, saucers and beer tankards.

Fruit trees. Apple, pear and plum are trees that usually give a hard and rather heavy-handed carving experience. The trees are usually twisted and knotty, making it more difficult to cleave them. However, one suitable use that takes advantage of the hard wood is to make a wooden mallet that you can use with an axe to split trunks.

A fancier fruit tree for carving is the wild cherry, or sweet cherry, as it is also called. It grows wild and resembles other cherry variants. The wood is softer than other fruit trees, and it is easy to cleave. The wood is a beautiful red in the core and lighter towards the taproot wood. Sometimes the color contrast is really great, which can produce nice effects.

Fir. The fir is a very common tree and is often used for newspaper production. The grain is knottier than pine and the fir has many small, hard twigs. The fir needs a lot of winters to get strong. You can tell how fast a fir grew from the distance between the annual rings, where the dark edge shows resin; the closer to-gether, the stronger the wood. The light and somewhat soft wood has been used for violin making, but even if you are not going to carve a Stradivarius, it can be good as a handle for a broom.

Laburnum. Laburnum or golden chain is actually in the pea family, so it may seem strange that it is included in this tree collection. The reason is, of course, that the wood is really cool to carve with and can produce a beautiful color scheme. The laburnum is poisonous, so carving this wood can be considered an exercise for the brave. Sawdust and shavings can irritate allergies, and we cannot recommend using laburnum for food utensils.

Hazel. The hazel tree grows differently compared to other trees. The shoots sprout close to each other and form a dense, bush-like group of straight, slender trunks without many branches – in other words, perfect to use for carving. The wood is quite soft and leathery, which does not hurt either. The medullary rays can often be seen clearly. Hazel wicker is tough and flexible and has historically been used for basket weaving and barrel binding. Most hazel trees are quite small, but there are also older specimens that are fairly large. An unusual characteristic of the hazelnut is that it blossoms with tiny flowers on its bare twigs as early as March or April.

→→

1.

2.

5.

8.

3.

4.

TREE TYPES

1. Alder
2. Ash
3. Pear
4. Pine
5. Walnut
6. Juniper
7. Fir
8. Maple
9. Linden

6.

7.

9.

Linden. Linden trees can be real giants of up to 30 meters tall, and their life spans can be as long as an entire millennium. The wood is soft and straight – it's no wonder that the linden is a favorite of craftsmen. For structures that will need to withstand high stress, it is too soft and light, but as a carving material, linden is very nice. In the cross section, it is difficult to distinguish the pith from the taproot.

Maple. Maple is autumn's star tree with its crackling leaves in yellow and red. The wood from the maple is quite hard and has pretty annual rings and visible medullary rays, so it's a popular craft material – even though it is relatively difficult to cleave. Traditionally, maple has been used for furniture but also ladles and other household items.

Pine. Pine wood is reddish brown, and its heartwood contains a lot of resin – that's why so much soot is produced when you burn it. It is this amount of resin that also makes the pine quite reddish. On a pine stump, the rings are clearly visible: spring's rings are light and the rings of autumn are darker and more sap-filled.

A pine that grows in an exposed place, for example by the sea, becomes gnarled and windblown and is sometimes called dwarf pine. Even pines that grow less exposed are often twisted – making them harder to cleave nicely. Traditionally, pine has been used in Sweden for houses, boatbuilding and simple furniture.

Walnut. Walnut does not really grow wild in Sweden, but has sometimes gone wild from cultivated specimens. In order to find fresh walnut to carve, you need luck, but you can buy walnut wood from well-stocked lumber yards or in handicraft shops. Walnut is a common wood used in interior decorating. The wood is quite hard to carve, but produces amazing color.

X

PART 2 ✕ WOOD CARVING

Moa's sense of wood

"I think it's great for people to carve. Just feeling their fingers do something that they are told to do – more than clicking on a keyboard or a phone. I think the connection between the brain and the hands is more important than we think."

Furniture maker and fine carpenter Moa Brännström Ott often gets going with a carving knife in her hand – and the hours fly by without her noticing. Thoughts clear as shavings dance to the floor. And when she's done, there's something concrete left.

"When I carve, it is only the here and now that means something. It is full concentration, but at the same time there is a calmness in the body, a feeling that it can take the time it takes. You cannot set a deadline for carving something. It's done when it's done – a few days or three weeks, you cannot say in advance. It's not me who decides how long it will take or when it's ready. It's the hands that decide."

Moa's hands live their own lives. The image she has in her head and what her hands do with the knife do not always match. For example, she sometimes thinks of an end result with a coarser, larger surface – but her hands continue to carve smaller and smaller, and the blank becomes thinner and thinner, until she almost stops carving and instead "mostly sits and feels with her fingers."

"It's so awesome, that I might want to make a certain expression but then my hands do something different."

Form-wise, she begins without limitations. She does not sketch or measure, but goes on feeling the whole way. Often there are spoons and *guksi* cups, probably because they offer varied carving with both sweeping lines and hollowing. And then, they will not get done so quickly.

$\longrightarrow$

*"I've always had it a lot easier with the three-dimensional than the two-dimensional.
I've always been very bad at drawing. It's really funny because I am so clumsy and
not at all in control of my limbs – I knock over glasses, walk into chairs and doorways
all the time – nevertheless, I can make really delicate items, or furniture that's perfect
in ten parts."*

In her opinion, Moa was quite inattentive and did poorly at school, and school
fatigue meant that she was looking for something more handy to do with herself.
She found it at Södertörn's Free Handicraft Gymnasium, and basically every day
since then, she has been devoted to wood. It's not really strange, she says.

"I've had a sense of wood ever since I was little. I even collected sticks.
I carved at my mother's house, and there were always wood chips on the floor in
the kitchen."

Moa's mother is an artist and had an understanding for creativity. After high
school, Moa tried out pottery at Nyckelviks School of Art for one year. The clay
was lovely, but Moa realized that she was only using a carving technique on the
clay. She would form something, allow it to dry until it was leather dry, and then
she mostly carved – so she figured she might as well work with wood instead.

Moa continued her education for three years at Capellagården in Öland,
Sweden. A cocky 19-year old punk girl collided with a world of full beards and
Birkenstock shoes – but she fell in love with the place and Carl Malmsten's spirit
floating high above it all.

"What I really got from Capellagården is respect for the material. To be with
it the whole way: from picking out and chopping down a tree, sawing it up into
boards and then making furniture out of it. Then wood becomes so much more
than just a board. We had a teacher who told us that before chopping down
a tree, we should give it a hug and promise to do something good with it. That
is beautiful. When I go into the woods, I usually talk to them and hug them – if
people could see me, they would probably think I was crazy."

Moa's family originates from Västerbotten, and Moa has spent a lot of time
on the farm outside Storuman. Her great-grandmother was a real craftswoman,

so handicraft has always been around in her family. For Moa, going to the workshop to chop, carve and saw was the most natural thing. If there is something she misses living in Stockholm, it is just to go out and saw down a birch and carve something. But not having her own forest in Stockholm does not hinder Moa.

"I often pick up wood I find around town. Trees are taken down quite often, and they are already cut into proper pieces. I have a balcony bench full of sticks and branches I picked up in town."

A tree that Moa was crazy about for a while was ginkgo, also called Chinese temple trees – a nice tree with beautiful two-lobed leaves that are seldom planted in Sweden. One day when Moa rode to work along Hornsgatan – where the city actually planted a handful of ginkgo trees – she suddenly saw a garbage truck drive into one of the trees and break it. Moa raced to work and called Stockholm's Department of Public Works. Would it be okay if she took care of the tree? "People are already on their way to haul it away," they replied. Moa fetched a saw and ran back to guard the tree while she harassed the bureaucrat on the phone to find someone who could alter the fate of the tree. In the end she got her way, and the unlucky ginkgo ended its days as spoons and salad utensils shaped like ginkgo leaves – instead of being ground into sawdust.

"A large part of the finished object is the link I have with the tree that the wood came from. Where it grew and how I overcame it. The object becomes something more than just a coffee mug, it also becomes a memory of a certain tree and a certain day. It seems strange to me to buy wood. I do not carve a spoon because I need a spoon. I carve for the sake of carving."

Ginkgo-shaped spoons are not typical in the Swedish carving tradition, but Moa also thinks that the fairly similar Swedish craft technique may need to be updated:

"In Sweden, it's about carving objects that have a certain expression, an expression that recurs, no matter who is carving it. It will not be so inspiring in the long run. So, it's good that new things start happening now."

Moa usually does not sand the carved surface – it's mostly burls and the inside of spoons that ever get to meet sandpaper. The carved object's surface of small marks from the knife represent all of its power. It would be a shame to sand away all the effort, she thinks. Moa does carving not only at her workbench in the living room or in front of the television – with her craft bag, she has everything she needs accompanying her everywhere:

$\longrightarrow\longrightarrow$

"I always take my craft bag when I'm traveling. It has compartments for knives, a small folding saw, whetstones and even a carving blank finds room. I have everything together in it so that I can sit and make something anywhere – on the train I usually feel the most nervous, where there is a greater risk of being thrown off if you're sitting with a knife."

Today, Moa works frequently as a fine carpenter to Uglycute Design Agency and helps with carpentry in connection with exhibitions and artistic works. But in the long term, her dreams for the future do not involve Stockholm.

"I dream of moving sometime to a farm in Norrland, having a carpentry workshop, a herd of goats and a dog. I don't want to stay in Stockholm. I think it's too complicated to live in town – there are too many steps to everything. I want to put my feet right in the grass when I go outside, and have twenty steps to the workshop. Be able to go cut down a birch and carve something. Here in Stockholm, carving becomes a link to that life. I do not understand how people can live here without a carpentry bench in the living room. I have to be close to something to do things. I must be able to cut off a stick. Otherwise I'd go crazy."

X

Carving star from another century

Once upon a time there was a Swedish carver who was a super celebrity. Under the artist name Döderhultaren, Axel Pettersson was widely talked about in the early 1900s – his name came from the village he was born in. As a young Bohemian, Döderhultaren depicted the personalities that he came in contact with in Oskarshamn. The clergyman, the clockmaker, the lecturer and other members of the small community saw themselves portrayed in the distinctive style of Döderhult. He was eventually discovered and was able to exhibit around the country and as far away as New York and San Francisco.

Döderhultaren carved his works in alder and used saw, axe, knife and different chisels. He worked in relatively fresh wood, and it is not uncommon for his figures to have cracks. He made his shapes rough and coarse, liked to saw and break out details to get another surface and did not care to carve away the saw cuts. His black jacket was heavily worn over his chest where he leaned on the blank while he was carving. He often carved arms, shoes and accessories like accordions, chairs, sticks and umbrellas separately and then glued them onto his figures.

In Oskarshamn's cultural house there is a permanent exhibition about Döderhultaren – if you get a chance, visit the exhibition for inspiration for your own works. Almost more impressive than his old men and women are the animals. His work, *Apocalypse*, for example, portraying ravenous horses running off a cliff, is nothing short of magnificent. Making images of animals was also safer than depicting people.

X

A carving club on the island

On a farm in Väskinde, one of Gotland, Sweden's 92 parishes, there is a warm boiler room with a few chairs placed around a chopping block. Tools hang in rows along the walls, and a few nights a month the floor gets covered with fresh shavings. Artist Shelley Sharr acts as host to the recurring gathering, which consists of a handful of middle-aged men who try to meet regularly to drink tea and carve. Most find themselves in the same place: with children who have left the home and a working life that rolls on. In the boiler room, the views expand again.

"At this stage of life, new questions emerge when life is not dictated by children and family in the same way anymore. You realize that you have twenty good years in front of you and you want to do something good with it," says Ruben Persson, sculptor and gardener.

There are many depths in the group's carving, says Shelley. The actual handicraft, or "doing" as he calls it, may not be the main point for all of them.

"Actually, the most important part are the thoughts that are awakened, all the conversations that get started. Our discussions here can cover any topic whatsoever. There is no subject we have not touched on here in the boiler room."

Ruben continues.

"Having something in your hands makes the discussion natural, unforced. One can just lean back and relax while carving. Had we just met to talk, I would probably have felt pressured – now the conversation suddenly just takes direction instead."

The participants have different intentions with the carving club. For some, it is the social part that is important, a little bubble in everyday life that gives us a place to see each other. For others, like Ruben, it is also an opportunity to really get engaged in wood carving.

$\longrightarrow\longrightarrow$

"To just sit and talk, I probably would not give myself time for that. As far as the carving is concerned, I am particularly interested in the scale shift. Otherwise, I work with big wooden constructions, but the wood fibers work the same way in a small stick as in a large log, so if I can do something on a small scale, then it's technically possible to do it on a large scale too."

Today, Shelley is carving on a long birch piece. Asked what it will become, he answers: "It's a must-have stick":

"I once had a teacher at folk high school who said, 'Go out into the woods, pick something up, and carve anything.' He called it carving a fool-stick. That's what's nice with wood as a material. It directly creates a spontaneous and creative feeling. Wood is a material that inspires. How much people work with it and in what context, it still works. To me, wood is a significant source of concentrated inspiration."

Wood seems to be a good material to bring out the thoughts of those at the club gathering. Wood is not just creativity, but also therapy, culture and politics. Ruben explains:

"At the bottom there is a do-it-yourself thing, to see opportunities to solve problems with the given material and your own hands. Then art and artistry come in, and there is also the therapeutic part – how the craft helps to make the days feel meaningful. And politically, wood crafting raises questions about materialism and consumption; wood is everywhere, and you can do anything in theory, but much of it is just lying rotting in the woods – or, at best, it will be sawdust. It's nice to try to take care of it, making creation a basic principle."

X

PART 3 ✕ PROJECTS

Butter knives and spatulas

Few items are as associated with woodworking as the butter knife. Hannes made his first butter knife in third grade – a piece of juniper wood was worked with a coping saw, file, and sandpaper in three different sizes. It took a long time, almost half a semester, and after cleaning and sanding for several classes, the shape was finally so vague that you could hardly see a difference between the handle and the blade. Ten years later, Hannes made a butter knife again. This time he used fresh birch, with an axe and knife as tools, and it went much faster.

Many people think a butter knife should be made with juniper. Juniper is a beautiful wood that smells good, resists moisture and cures well. It is also a bush, which means that the wood is full of twigs. The stem is seldom round and smooth; instead it is wavy and the wood is often twisted as if the whole bush rotated slowly while growing. All in all, that makes juniper a bad choice for someone who is carving for the first time. Instead, choose a blank from some straight and knot-free deciduous tree, preferably fresh. It also works well with a piece of birch.

With the knives you buy, the handle and blade are often thick. If you make the handle at least twice as thick as the blade, the knife becomes much more stable. Of course you can oil your finished butter knife, but otherwise the butter will grease it anyway.

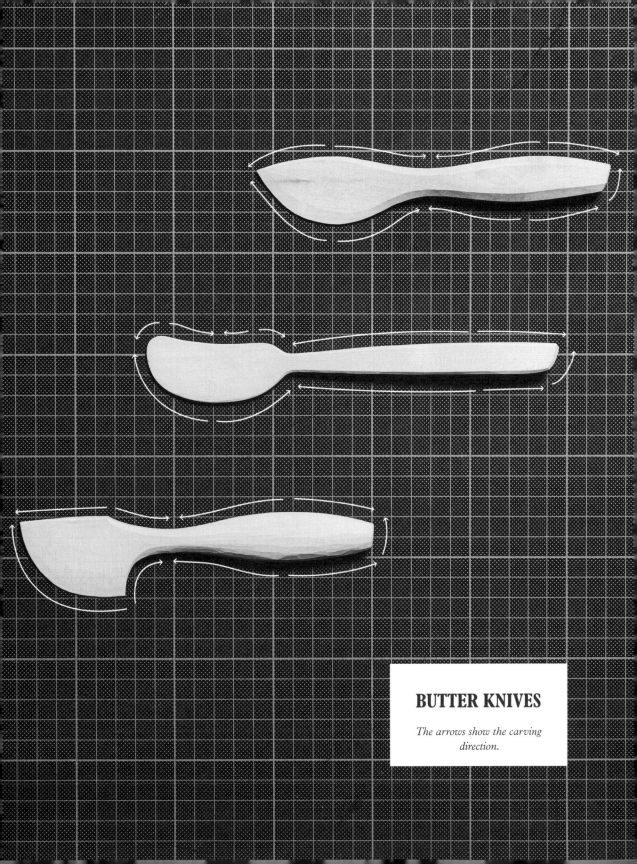

BUTTER KNIVES

The arrows show the carving direction.

BUTTER KNIFE

Fresh or dry straight wood • axe • knife

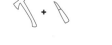

DO IT THIS WAY

1. Cleave a rectangular blank that is straight and knot-free, approximately 20 × 5 × 1.5 cm. Smooth the surfaces with the axe. Sketch the shape of the knife directly onto the wooden piece with a pencil. Try to sketch the knife shape to follow the fibers in the wood as much as possible. This makes it easier to cut out the shape with the axe.

2. Rough out the shape with the axe. Remove a little material at a time and dare to axe your way up to the lines. Cut in the direction of the grain, not against – otherwise the wood will split.

3. Carve the butter knife's outlines with the knife. Shape the butter knife: Make the handle thick and then cut thinner toward the blade. Carve down the blade's back until it is 3–4 mm thick and then thin it down so that the butter knife gets a clear edge. Let the butter knife remain angular until you have both sides equal and you are satisfied with the proportions. If you start rounding off before then, carving a bit here and a bit there, it's easy to lose the shape.

4. Finally, shape the handle and bevel the edges of it to make the butter knife comfortable to hold.

TIPS!

As a beginner, you have the
greatest chance of success
if you go systematically.
Take a moment before
moving on to the next part.

Spatula › When you start carving, a fun first goal is to replace all the ugly plastic tools with hand-carved wooden varieties. In order for the spatula's blade to be as strong and durable as possible, the rings should lie horizontally on the blade. The annual rings are more horizontal the farther from the pith you go, so in this case it is better to use a blank from a larger tree.

SPATULA

Fresh wood piece • knife • saw • axe

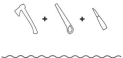

DO IT THIS WAY

Your blank should be about 35 × 5 × 4 cm. Cut the blank so that the handle is closest to the bark.

Begin by flattening to the side that will be the bottom of the spatula. Sketch the spatula's profile directly onto the wood piece. The spot where the handle and the blade meet is the weakest point of the spatula, so make sure the handle and blade overlap properly so that the grain fibers do not get too short where they meet. Keep in mind that some of the handle disappears in the bend, so do not make the handle too short. Cut down to the stop cut and split the spatula's handle and blade with the ax. When you have axed out the shape roughly level to the transitions, thin the blade with the knife before allowing the blank to dry. If your wood is already fairly dry, you can proceed to the next step immediately.

When your blank is dry, you are ready to shape the spatula. Thin down the blade further so that the thickest spot in the middle of the blade is about 5–6 mm and the outer edges are 1–2 mm.

Shape the handle and bevel the edges slightly so that it feels good in your hand.

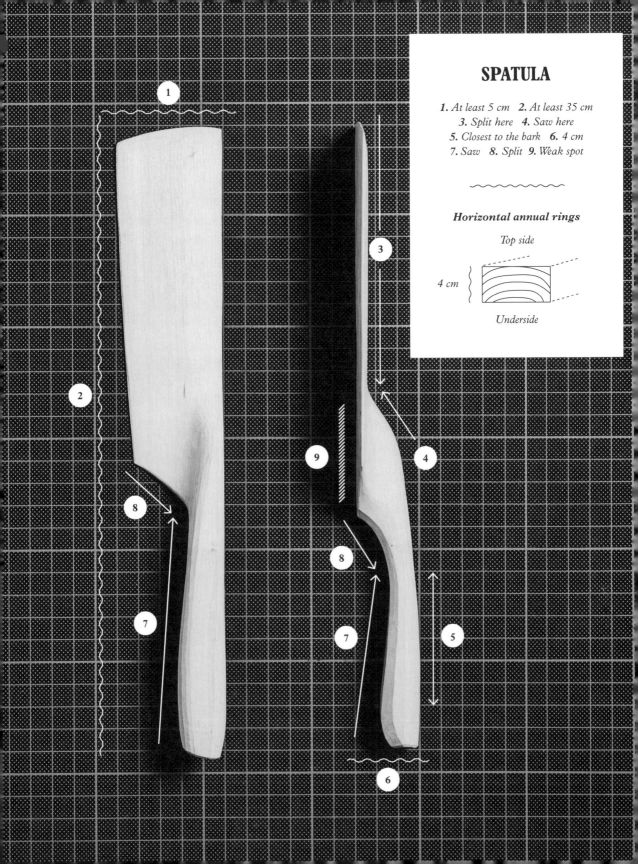

SPATULA

*1. At least 5 cm   2. At least 35 cm
3. Split here   4. Saw here
5. Closest to the bark   6. 4 cm
7. Saw   8. Split   9. Weak spot*

Horizontal annual rings

Top side

4 cm

Underside

Spoons, ladles and scoops

Metal spoons first appeared in most homes in the early 1900s. Before that, carved spoons were everyday utensils, and they were personal – everyone in the family had their own spoon.

A rack was used to hang up wooden spoons in the farmhouse. During harvest time, when there were many people on the farm, the rack was filled with spoons – and thus one had a full house.

Spoon or ladle > Traditional ladle connoisseurs prefer to make their ladles from a crooked blank, that is, a piece of wood with a natural bend. Of course, it is best if the fibers of the wood are unbroken throughout the entire neck from the handle and even into the blade, but it is not a must, at least not if you are going to make a ladle with only a weak S-curve. By creating the ladle diagonally on the blank, even in straight wood, you can make a utensil that will serve you for many years to come.

If you cut a blank from fresh wood, it is best to make the ladle so that the top of the handle is closest to the bark. Then the hollowing out of the ladle's bowl will pull together when the ladle dries – the ladle will become more bowl-shaped when dry. If you reverse the ladle so the bowl is closest to the bark, when you dig out on the opposite side the ladle's bowl will become flatter during drying. If you use a log that has been sitting out and drying for a while, the ladle will remain largely as you carved it, no matter how much you hollow out the blank.

~~~~~~~~~~

SPOON OR LADLE

**Fresh wood piece • knife
spoon gouge • saw • axe**

~~~~~~~~~~

DO IT THIS WAY

1. To make a ladle, you need a blank that is about 30 × 8 × 4 cm. Smooth the long sides with the axe and draw the ladle's profile on each side. The weakest point of the ladle is on the underside where the handle meets the ladle's bowl. Make the ladle a bit thicker here.

2. Axe out the profile. If you want, you can saw some stop cuts to facilitate breaking out. Axe as close to the lines as you dare.

3. Draw the ladle from above.

4. Here too, the use of the axe can be made easier by sawing across on each side of the bridge, or where the bowl of the ladle and the handle meet.

5. Axe out the shape. Round the ladle's bottom slightly with the axe.

$\longrightarrow\longrightarrow$

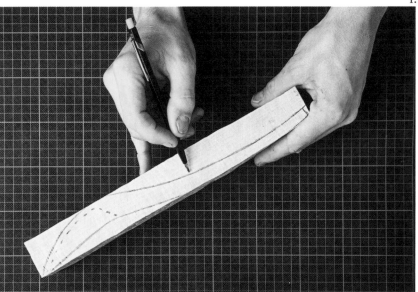

6.

7.

8.

9.

6. Even up the transitions between the handle and the bowl with the knife.

7. Now it's time to dig out the ladle. Draw the ladle's inner form and dig out the ladle's bowl with the spoon gouge. When you work your way down the ladle, you can carve from all directions and edges toward the center. The ladle should be the deepest closest to the handle.

8. When you're happy with the inside, adjust the outside. If you're working with fresh wood, let the ladle dry before continuing.

9. When the ladle has dried, fix up the shape and carve a nice surface. When you carve the inside of the bowl, you have to carve with the grain direction to get a clean cut and a nice surface. To see which grips are suitable, see page 33. Round the handle so that it fits well in your hand and bevel the edges slightly; a rounded handle lasts longer with wear and tear than one with sharper edges.

TIPS!

It may be a good idea to draw a line down the center of the ladle. This makes it easier to get the ladle symmetrical than if eyeballing it.

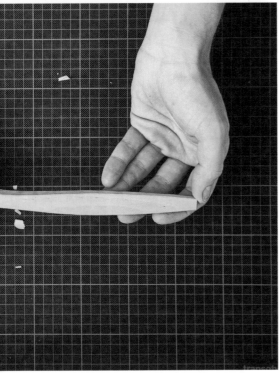

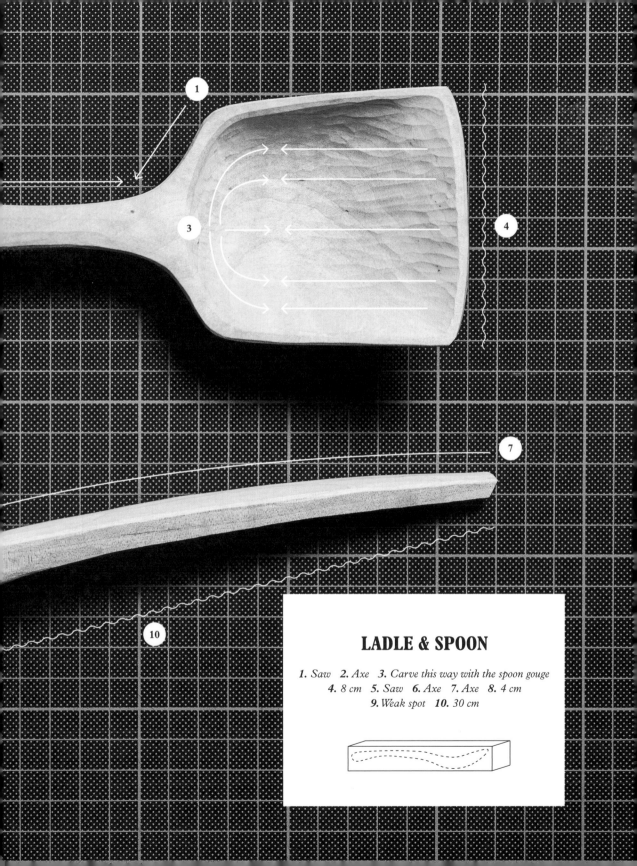

LADLE & SPOON

1. Saw   *2.* Axe   *3.* Carve this way with the spoon gouge
4. 8 cm   *5.* Saw   *6.* Axe   *7.* Axe   *8.* 4 cm
9. Weak spot   *10.* 30 cm

Scoop > Carved scoops are nice and useful, perfect for scooping up muesli or flour and giving your kitchen the nice vibe of an old-time farmstead.

Shape the blank according to the size of your intended scoop. Use a straight, untwisted piece of wood and avoid the grain. If you shape the blank so that the scoop's opening will be against the bark, it will contract inward during drying.

SCOOP

Fresh wood piece • knife
spoon gouge • saw • axe

DO IT THIS WAY

Cleave out a square blank and smooth out what will be the top of the scoop.

Draw out how the scoop should look from above and from the side on the blank.

Make a cut from the bottom up to the handle and cleave away excess wood.

Saw a cut from the side into the place where the bowl and handle of the scoop will meet. Break out the handle.

Round the bottom of the scoop roughly with the axe.

Draw the inner shape of the scoop. Dig out the scoop's bowl with the spoon gouges. If it is a larger sized scoop, it may be a good idea to use work gloves.

Once you have hollowed out the bowl, you can fine carve the scoop. The point at which bowl and handle meet is the weakest point, so do not make the scoop too thin here.

When the scoop looks basically the way you want it, let it dry.

Shape the scoop so that it has a nice surface. Make the handle nice to hold and bevel the edges slightly so that the scoop is better resistant to wear and tear.

Measuring cup set and coffee measure > It's really just the depth of the bowls that separates a measuring spoon from a ladle or spoon. You just need a bigger blank and a little more time for the larger items. A shortcut may be to drill down into the bowl using an egg cup drill bit, otherwise it will be just a matter of carving with the spoon gouge. It's always good to save material so that you can match the outside after you have finished carving the inside. If you're making a measuring spoon or cup that will hold an exact amount, it is good to go a little over the rim when you hollow out the blank and make the handle a little thicker. Once the blank has dried, you can fine carve the inside. If it's a measuring cup that you're making, drop in the desired amount of coffee powder and draw a line at that level. Then drop down to the line and thin the shaft so that the proportions are correct and everything is peace and joy.

Guksi or kåsa

The step from measurement scoop to guksi cup is not that far, at least not if you look at the approach. But a guksi is not just any cup, so to get a closer look at the history and tradition of this enchanting drink vessel, we talked to Gunnar Östman Inga to learn more. Gunnar has worked for the Sami Cultural Foundation, Sámi Duodji, in Jokkmokk, Sweden, and has been making guksi for a long time.

__Where does the name come from?__
In Norwegian it's called kosa with o. Kosa comes from the Sami word guksi. The guksi was originally a utility item, which people made themselves from what they had around them, like wood, horns and skins. It was all about self-sufficiency.

What kind of wood should you use to make the guksi?
- A guksi cup is almost always made of birch, and it should also be made with a burl (which are commonly found on birch trees). The ring of the burl goes around the guksi so it does not have end grain. That way you have a durable container that will hold hot water and coffee. You can also find burls for sale, but they often have black twist holes in them called black eyes, which means they can't hold liquid. Never make a guksi with pine because the pine leaves a strong taste.

Do you have to fell the tree to get to the burl?
- Usually if it's a small burl you can take it directly off the tree, but if you want a handle on your guksi cup then you should take part of the trunk too. Saw a cut above the burl and one underneath. Take extra wood from either side so you get a handle blank, and then just cut it out with the axe. Try to make as little impact as possible so it's easier for the tree to recover.

So you cannot make many guksi if you find a giant burl?

- The difference between Sami guksi and others is that we make them round, so you want to start from a round burl. You can make a bowl or a *nahppi*, which is a milk cup, from bigger burls. It should be a bit more closed at the top so the milk does not splash out if the reindeer moves when you milk it (though there are not many who milk reindeer by hand today).

How do you get started when making a guksi?

- Hollow out the blank when it is fresh. It is important to only allow the blank to dry slowly under controlled conditions. Put the blank in a plastic bag with newspaper. Every other day, remove the blank and turn the bag inside out so that you remove the condensation. Take out the newspaper and put in new dry newspaper. Do not take the blank directly into the heated house, but store it in a cool, shady place so it will get used to it gradually.

Traditionally, you use a hollow iron to dig out the guksi. It's like a spoon gouge except it has a ring instead of a hook, and you only need one to get in at any angle. The blade is forged in the middle and has an edge. It is maybe 8 cm long and bowed around so that both ends go into the handle. A modern variant of the hollow iron is the Dalsland iron, a small hand tool that is divine to work with and goes through the bottom almost at once. But today it is often a milling machine that is used to do the job.

Is it important that a guksi can stand by itself?

- A guksi is made to stand on uneven surfaces and not on flat tables, so a guksi should always have a round bottom. In huts there were always birch twigs and leaves on the floor, and the guksi is round-bottomed so it can stand anywhere, which a flat-bottomed guksi cannot do. However, if the guksi is well-balanced, it can stand on the table even if it has a round bottom.

Should there be a long or short handle on the guksi?

- It differs from area to area. In the northern Sami area of Sweden – Gällivare/ Kiruna and northward – the guksi have a shorter handle and are rounder in shape, almost a bit spherical. Often the handle is reinforced with a reindeer antler horn mount that is decorated with a floral, star or bloom-like pattern.

In the southern Sami area of Sweden – from Arvidsjaur/Arjeplog and southward – the guksi is less deep and flatter in shape. The handle is a bit longer and the horn plating has a different type of decor. The patterns are usually geometric and cover more or less the entire surface. In the central Sami area, Lulesami, the guksi is in between the other forms.

Do you sand the guksi?

- Guksi have had smooth surfaces for as long as can be. You can use sand even when you don't have any sandpaper. Carve as finely as possible, and at the end you can scrape with the knife to make it really smooth before starting to sand. In the south, they used to sand with scouring rush or horsetail, a plant.

What do you use for surface treatment on your guksi?

- A guksi must be completely untreated inside. On the outside you can use oil, either paraffin or cold pressed raw linseed oil. Historically guksi have been tinted with natural colors derived from sources such as willow and alder bark. Guksi was always treated on the outside, because dirt shows right away on white birch.

How do you care for your guksi?

- Wash it, but do not use detergent, just rinse it with water. If have you eaten out of it, use warm water. The best guksi is the one that can be used as a coffee cup and food bowl. I myself have two of them, of which the coffee aroma escapes from the larger guksi, which is also a food bowl. In the old days, you tucked it into your chest, and with the tunic belted, the guksi served as a pocket inside the tunic. Guksi cups are personal. You do not use someone else's guksi unless you are invited.

X

Kåsa › Even if the best guksi is made of a burl, it is possible to use a regular piece of wood as well. However, a guksi made of straight wood will not be as resistant and can crack if you have liquid in it for too long. Nevertheless, it can serve as a nice cup to take with you on a trip while waiting for that perfect burl to cross your path.

GUKSI

**Fresh wood piece • knife
spoon gouge • saw • axe**

DO IT THIS WAY

To make a guksi, you need a heavy piece of fresh wood without knots or pith. Birch is a good choice as it is a homogeneous wood that is not too hard. Cleave out a blank that is about 17 × 10 × 9 cm.

Sketch the guksi cup directly onto the blank. Saw and chop to roughly shape it, then start digging it out. Use gloves to avoid blisters on your hands, and store the blank in the refrigerator wrapped in a wet towel when you take a break.

When the hollowing-out is done, adjust the outside based on the shape of inside and, finally, shape the handle. Carve the guksi cup until it's almost ready, but leave a few millimeters for the fine shaping before letting the guksi cup dry slowly.

When the guksi is dry, carve cleanly for final shaping inside and outside. The inside should be sanded so that the fibers are clogged and the wood will absorb less liquid. Start with an 80 grit sandpaper and sand each side until the inside is smooth and fine. If you plan to stain it, do so before you treat the guksi's exterior with oil, and be sure to stain only the outside – the inside is left natural and untreated.

X

Espresso cup

The espresso cups shown in the picture are made of end grain. Carving into it with a knife is almost impossible; even if you can do it, it is guaranteed to be laborious and boring. However, you can drill down into the wood and then carve with a spoon gouge from the bottom up without much effort. You can use an egg cup drill bit, which almost feels wrong to recommend – it's difficult to control and it moves around and tears up the subject. The wood starts to smoke, the battery runs out and the result looks a bit pathetic. But after a few digs with the spoon gouge, the fine wood has been restored again, saving both time and the spoon gouge's sharpness.

The risk is high that a cup made of straight wood will split if it is left filled with liquid for too long. To be safe, you should wipe it out after it has been used. Of course, you do not have to make your espresso cup in end grain – a smaller model of the guksi is excellent for drinking strong coffee.

ESPRESSO CUP

**Fresh wood piece • drill
sanding cloth • saw • clamp
axe • egg cup drill bit**

DO IT THIS WAY

Cleave out a blank that is a few inches wider and longer than your cup will be. Smooth it with the axe so that the clamp can get a good grip on the blank. Clamp the blank and drill a hole that's approximately 3–4 cm deep.

When the egg cup drill bit has finished wreaking havoc, you can cleave off some of the excess wood to make it easier to hold the blank when carving the inside. However, it is not wise to chop off too much, as it is better to adjust the outside after you hollow out the inside than vice versa. Do not forget to save some wood for the handle.

When you've finished hollowing out the inside, start shaping the outside. The bottom should be sawed so that it is approximately 8 mm thick. Carve the handle and thin down the sides until they are approximately 6 mm thick. Allow the cup to dry.

When the cup is dry, start to do the fine shaping: First, make the bottom flat using the knife and then the sanding cloth. When the cup stands steady, even up the top; the easiest is to use the same trick as you would use for the shrink box (step 10 on page 104).

Be sure you shape the inside of the cup first, and then do the outside.

Since cut surfaces leave the pores of the wood open, the pores easily absorb moisture. But when you sand the inside, you block the pores so the wood absorbs less. Start with a sanding cloth that has 80 or 100 grit. When the inside feels smooth, change to a finer sandpaper. You can sand as long as you want or have patience for.

Treat the outside of the cup with oil; leave the inside untreated.

For a description of how to make the saucer, see page 116. The recess for the cup is done last. Place the cup on the saucer and draw around the shape. Hold the knife like a pencil and make a vertical cut with the tip of the knife along the line. Cut with the grain and push with the other hand's index finger. Gouge out the cut from the center with the knife or spoon gouge until the cup sits well in the recess. Treat the saucer with oil.

Wooden forks, chopsticks and salad utensils

DO IT THIS WAY

Chop a rectangular blank for your intended wooden fork. Avoid branches and the pith of the tree. The thickness should be at least 1 cm and the width should be at least 4–5 cm in order for this to be a usable tool. The length can be adjusted to your liking, but about 30 cm will usually be fine.

Saw and cut out the handle and thin down the blank slightly along the handle. Refine the shape of the fork.

Saw around the fork's teeth. Keep in mind not to saw the cuts too deep on the teeth that are outermost or they will break off easily. If the gap between the fork's teeth is wider than the saw's cut, you can drill a hole of appropriate thickness at the bottom of the teeth and then saw one or two cuts down to the hole.

If you're working with fresh wood, let the blank dry before continuing.

Use the knife to finely carve between the fork's teeth and shape the handle so that it will feel nice to hold.

Chopsticks > Chopsticks have been used in practically all of eastern Asia for the last 6,000 years. Today, they are close to an environmental problem because they are often disposable; in Japan alone, about 4.5 billion pairs of chopsticks are used per year. We could break this negative cycle if everyone carved their own chopsticks. The chance that you would want to throw them away after a meal is small, considering it's more time-consuming and meticulous to make your own chopsticks than you can imagine.

The length of chopsticks varies from country to country. Most often they are 20–25 cm long and made of bamboo, but some are made of wood, plastic, and porcelain. Chinese chopsticks differ from those made in Japan and Korea. Japanese chopsticks are shorter (18–21 cm), rounder and have prettier ends compared to the Chinese (23–26 cm), which usually have a rectangular shape and a more blunt point. The part you hold in your hand should be 5–6 mm thick and the other end about 3 mm.

CHOPSTICKS

Dry wood piece • knife • axe

DO IT THIS WAY

Cleave blanks that are as thin as you can make them. You cannot get them as thin as you need with an axe, but try to get as close as possible. Thin down the blank with the knife until you reach the desired thickness. To keep the blank from getting too crooked it's good to have a straight reference guide nearby, for example, a ruler or table top. Finish by beveling the edges slightly.

Salad utensils › To make salad utensils, you will proceed in the same way as you do for a ladle. However, the blank does not have to be as thick since the utensil's bowls need not be angled in relation to the handle as on a ladle.

SALAD UTENSILS

Fresh wood piece • drill • knife
spoon gouge • saw • axe

DO IT THIS WAY

Follow the instructions for a ladle on page 78 all the way to the end.

When the utensils have dried and you have shaped them properly, drill a hole in the middle of the bowl area on both of them using a large spiral drill bit. Saw two cuts down to the hole of one utensil so that the slit becomes a fork with two teeth. Refine the shape with the knife and bevel the edges slightly. Carve the other utensil's hole to the desired size and shape, then bevel the edges slightly and treat it with oil.

Shrink boxes

Even the Vikings carved shrink boxes (*krympburk* in Swedish), and it's easy to understand why. Not only are shrink boxes practical, it's really a pleasure to carve those long corkscrew-curled shavings – even the novice can feel like a professional. A shrink box can be made by hollowing out a fresh branch or tree trunk, cutting a groove inside one end of the cylinder and fitting a dry piece of wood into the groove to serve as the bottom of the box. When the fresh wood dries, it shrinks around the dry bottom and you get a nice, tight box (if you are careful, otherwise you will get a nice box that is not so tight – which is fine, too). The bottom must be cut along the grain, and you cannot use a slab of end grain for the bottom, as it will split during drying.

 If you do not have dry wood, you can quick-dry a blank in the oven overnight. Place the blank on the rack, set the oven to 100 degrees Farenheit and wedge a wooden ladle in the oven door to allow the moisture to escape. Make sure the blank is bigger than you will need – both in height and length – so that you can saw off any splits and plane out the piece when it is dry.

If you need a break when working, wrap the blank in a damp towel and put it all in the fridge. It is important that the fresh wood does not start to shrink before the bottom of dry wood is in place.

$\longrightarrow\longrightarrow$

You can also make square shrink boxes – it's just a little more work than making round ones.

SHRINK BOX

**Fresh branch or dry trunk wood
piece • drill with 10–15 mm
drill bit • knife spoon gouge
axe • chisel (opt.)**

THE BLANK

Your blank will be easier to carve if you choose one from a deciduous tree that is straight, even and knot-free. Make sure the blank is a centimeter longer than you want the box to be when it is finished. You can leave the bark on or remove it with the axe.

It does not take long after a tree or branch has been cut before it begins to split at the saw cut. Some small cracks at the pith are okay – they will be cut away when you dig out the blank – but the parts that will be the sides of your box must be completely free from cracks. If your blank has started cracking, cut off a few decimeters to get raw wood with few or no cracks. If you have found a blank but do not have the time to start on it right away, you can put it in a little water to help prevent it from drying and splitting.

DO IT THIS WAY

1. Drill a hole all the way through the blank with the largest drill bit you have. A spiral drill is preferred when it comes to fresh wood. If you have a mortise chisel, you can drill several holes close to each other and break out the material between the holes.

2. Now it's time to hollow out the blank with the knife. If you're making a larger box, find a pair of work gloves to prevent blisters on your hands. Use a knife with a thin blade; a wider blade cuts at a steep angle and then the knife chops instead of cutting. If you're making a taller box, you'll need a long knife to get in far enough to hollow it out the whole way. A good technique when hollowing out a smaller blank is to hold the wood piece in your hand and twist the blank and the knife at the same time as you carve, much like wringing out a cloth.

3. Work alternately from each side and try to get the sides of the box as even as possible. A smaller box should have sides that are about 5–6 mm thick and a larger box should have sides that are 7–9 mm thick in order to be sturdy. A small box is easier to handle during the work process and can be thinner, while a larger box needs thicker sides to be stable. Finish by making sure that the bottom of the box will stand well on flat surfaces.

4.

5.

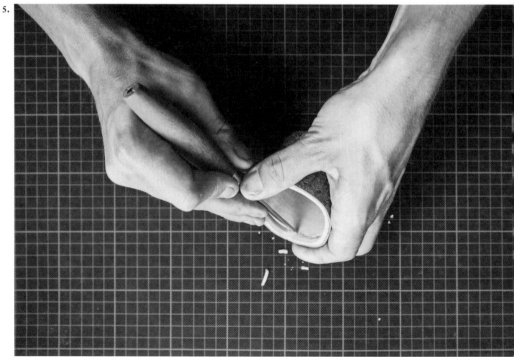

4. Draw a line around the inside of the cylinder, about 12 mm up from the bottom. Then draw another one about 4 mm underneath the first line so you have two parallel lines.

5. Cut with the tip of the knife along the upper line; the cut should be about 3 mm deep. Then, cut at an angle from the other line up to the first one. Clear out the wood in that section between the two lines with the tip of the knife to make a clean and clear V-shaped groove that runs around the entire cylinder.

6. Take a dry, knot-free blank to make the bottom of your shrink box. If you have a froe, it'll be most efficient to use that. Otherwise, cleave out your blank with a knife and wooden mallet or with the axe. It's good to have some extra wood so you don't have to chop close to your hands. Cut the right length with the saw, level it then cut a nice surface with the knife. Your bottom should be 4–6 mm thick.

7. Sharpen the pencil and place the cylinder onto the blank that will be the bottom of the box. Draw around the inside of the cylinder. Make marks in the cylinder and on the bottom so that you know how the pieces were placed when you drew around them. This will be helpful when you fit the bottom.

8. Saw out the rough shape of the bottom then use the knife to carve the last bit up to the line. When that is done, bevel the edge of the bottom. The beveling should fit into the groove you made in the cy-

linder. When the bottom is fitted, you can set the box someplace safe to dry. It will usually be dry in a few days, a little longer if you left the bark on. If you want the box to dry more slowly, you can put it on a shelf in the refrigerator.

9. When the box has dried properly and the cylinder has shrunk firmly around the bottom, start to even out the bottom of the box so it's flat on the underside. Cut off most of the uneven parts with the knife and remove the rest with the sanding cloth. Be sure to sand against a flat surface.

10. When the bottom of the box is flat, even up the top edge. A good trick to do that is to first draw a circle around the outside by laying a pen on something flat. In the picture, we put the pen on another shrink box but books are also a favorite since they are large enough to keep the pen steady and are different thicknesses. Make a pile of books that is high enough that the pen just reaches the lowest point on the box's upper edge. Hold the pen still and push the box onto the tip until you have a line that goes full circle. Cut down to the line with the knife.

If you removed the bark, you can fine carve the box on the outside so the wood has a luster. Inside, it can be difficult to get a really sharp cut even when the wood has dried – it's enough to bevel off the edge lightly and allow the inside to be a bit more rough.

SHRINK BOX

When you're going to hollow out a blank that is so big you cannot hold it in your hand, rest it on your thigh. When you hollow it out in this way, you need to dig in more so the pressure on the blank will increase. A blank with a larger diameter will also become softer and more flexible and should therefore have thicker sides so as not to break apart during work. A large cylinder also requires a large bottom. When the dry bottom is in place, it will push into the fresh wood as it dries, so during this time it's good to check that the bottom is shrinking into the groove as it should. Once the box has dried, you can thin the walls slightly if you want.

Lid for shrink wood box › The design of the lid is flexible enough that you can vary it according to your taste and style. What most lids have in common is that they are held in place by a lip, or rim, that matches the inner shape of the box and extends a few millimeters into the box.

DO IT THIS WAY

1. To make the lid, cut out a blank that is large enough to fit your box. Begin by smoothing what will be the underside of the lid with the knife. Place the shrink box on the blank and draw around the outside of it. You'll need to make the lid a bit wider than the box, so do not draw too close to the edge. Make markings on both the lid and the box so that you can find the same position again. Saw out a rough outline of the lid, then carve up to the lines with the knife.

2. Most people have probably taken an impression of a coin or leaf by placing it under a piece of paper and then rubbing over it with a pencil or chalk. The same trick can be used to get the exact size of the inside of the shrink box to design the inner rim to fit, but instead of putting pencil to paper, you blacken your finger with pencil lead and draw with that. Place the shrink box on the table and place a piece of paper on top. Draw with your finger until you get the shape of the inside of box on the paper. Cut the paper along the lines, lay the pattern on the blank and trace around it.

When you are going to do the rim, you start by drawing a line around the outer edges of the lid that shows the rim's depth, about 4–6 mm. There are a few different techniques you can use to carve out the rim. If you just want to use the knife, on the inside of the lid cut with the tip vertically along the line that shows the box's inner shape.

Then use the knife to remove the wood up to the cut from the side. Repeat this step around the entire lid. Even up the rim and keep making adjustments with the knife until the lid fits the box.

3. Another way to carve out the rim is to use the saw. To saw safely and precisely, use a clamp to clamp the blank to the table with the underside facing up. It is best to use a fine-toothed saw with a wide blade, preferably a Japanese saw. A tip to avoid sawing too deep is to put a tape strip on the saw blade that is the same distance from the end of the blade as the cut should be deep. Saw out vertical sections around the line showing the inner shape of the box. The more cuts you make, the less you need to carve.

$\longrightarrow\longrightarrow$

4. When you finish sawing, break out the rim from the side with the knife. Then, fine shape the rim with the knife and fit the lid.

5. If you want, you can dig out the underside of the lid with spoon gouges to trim the lid more. Start gouging a few millimeters from the rim so the lip isn't too flimsy.

6. Shape the top of the lid.

7. Bevel the edges

8. Surface treat the lid with oil.

If you do not want to dirty your finger with pencil lead and you have a scanner, you can put your shrink wood box upside down on the glass and allow the machine to photograph the inside of the box. Then print the image, cut out the inner shape with scissors, place it on the wooden piece that will become the lid, and draw around it. However, this is quite detailed and not very rock 'n' roll.

Clothes hook

 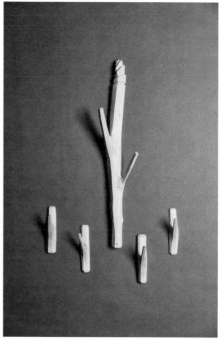

No wood composition is as strong as what the tree itself creates when it sends a branch out from its trunk. The crown of a tree is full of potential clothes hooks and utilizing tree crowns for such is an old trick. However, some blanks are better than others – if you find a tree where many branches crowd a small area, you should act on this opportunity. Sometimes you can find forests where the young trees have been thinned out and the fallen trees have just been left on the hillside. That's a golden opportunity to go out with the hedge clippers and botanize among the tree crowns. However, you may not always have such luck, and, as always, if you want to take down a tree, you must have the landowner's permission.

CLOTHES HOOK

Spiky branch • drill • knife
saw • axe

DO IT THIS WAY

Select a piece of wood to get started. Keep in mind that the blank makes the hook, so choose the wood with care.

Cut out the blank roughly and leave 5–6 extra cm at all ends. Keep in mind that the hook will need to be attached at both the top and bottom with nails or screws, so you must be able to reach those with a hammer or screwdriver, as appropriate.

Cleave away extra wood and roughly plane the back of the hook with the axe. When the blank has dried, the back will have curved and you will have to plane it again for it to fit well against the wall.

Roughly carve the hook and let it dry for a week or two. It's very likely that the hook will split at the ends, since the branches that still have pith are especially prone to splitting. However, the splits usually do not go farther than a few centimeters, so you can usually cut off the splits when you cut off the extra centimeters.

When you are carving your hook, you will need to use a lot of different grips. If you have a blank with many branches, the carving will be extra tricky because the branches make work difficult. You can try different grips to see which ones work best. Be extra careful at the area where the trunk and branch meet, since the grain of the wood changes direction there.

If you like, bevel the edges at the end of the hook, or spice it up with a knob or fancy carving.

Plane the back of the hook so it fits flush against the wall. Drill a hole for the screw or nail before you insert it so the wood doesn't split. If you do not want to use nails, there are different types of hangers that can be attached to the back of the hook.

Knobs and bling

Whether you want to make a ring or a door knob, or you just want to spice up a clothes hook or ladle handle, the approach is essentially the same. Not all knobs require that you use a saw, but it is always good to sketch an outline of the shape you'd like to have onto the blank so you have something to go by when carving.

Many prefer to carve a knob on the end of a longer blank and then cut the blank to the right length. A larger blank is easier to hold on to, which makes carving easier. The size of the blank will be dictated by the type of knob you want to carve, but starting from a square blank usually works well.

$\longrightarrow\longrightarrow$

~~~~~~~~~~~~~

KNOB

Dry wood piece • knife • saw • axe

~~~~~~~~~~~~~

DO IT THIS WAY

Knob › 1. Draw out the knob on one or more sides of your blank and draw lines around it as shown in the photo.

2. It will be easier to carve out the knob if you saw cuts around the blank that you cut against. Use a fine-toothed saw and put a piece of tape on the saw blade so you know how deep you should saw.

3. Carve and break out the shape of the knob. Make every side as even as possible. It's important to be careful here to get a good end result. Draw new lines around the knob that show where each bevel should begin and end.

4. Carve systematically and shape each bevel all the way around before starting a new one.

2.

4.

KNOB WITH SCREW

**Dry wood piece • drill • knife
screw • saw
two-part epoxy • axe**

⏉ + ⎯ + ⑃

~~~~~~~~~~

DO IT THIS WAY

Knob with screw > If you want to be on the safe side, begin by attaching the screw to the blank, before carving the knob. When you drill, you won't know for sure whether the hole will be exactly where you want it, and when you glue the screw, it can be difficult to know for sure that it will be completely straight in relation to the knob.

Start by drilling a hole in the blank that is big enough to hold the screw and deep enough that the head can be buried in glue. Glue the screw as straight as you can. When the glue is dried, straighten up the blank according to the screw. Before you start carving, tape around the screw so the threads are not destroyed if you should hit the screw with the knife. If you want, you can leave the blank on its standing edge so you have more to hold onto during work.

RING

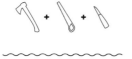

DO IT THIS WAY

Ring › Making a round ring that's made out of wood is tricky. No matter which way you turn the wood piece, you will not see where the short fibers are (unless you want a long wooden pipe on your finger) so the ring will be brittle. It is better to buy plain metal rings in the hobby shop and carve a handsome button that serves as the bling for your ring. Wood, of course, gives rings character and individuality. Branches, growths and even infestations can affect the wood and make for exciting blanks as the foundation for fancy rings, but even ordinary birch can be stylish in its simplicity.

The dark rings shown in the photo are made of a very hard, exotic wood; exactly which is hard to say. These wooden pieces come from a broken chair in the '50s style that was beyond all rescue.

When you're making a button for a ring, it is easier to carve the button from a longer blank and then cut off the excess when you're finished.

Most buttons are carved so that the top of the button is of end grain, but that's not a must. Some of the rings in the picture are carved so that the end grain is on the sides, which lends your ring a different look.

Treat the top of the button with oil but leave the surface that will be glued to the ring untreated so the two-part epoxy sticks properly. If you have made the bottom of the button arched, you may need to plane off the part that will be glued to the ring's body.

Bowl and saucer

If you're making a tray or a larger bowl, you need a tool sturdier than a spoon gouge for hollowing it out. For a smaller bowl or plate, however, a spoon gouge works very well. If the wood you're working with is really fresh, it does not take long to cut a bowl big enough to accommodate olives, rings or rubber bands. Put on work gloves so you will not get blisters on your hands. The approach is the same whether you're making a bowl or a saucer, so follow the instructions on the next page, and if you're making a saucer, substitute "saucer" for "bowl."

It's wise to hollow out from the bark toward the pith instead of the opposite, which may feel more logical. As the wood dries, the blank will warp inward, and you will have a deeper bowl when the blank is dry. The downside of doing it this way is your bowl will be smaller than what you started with. If you dig out from the core toward the bark, the opposite will happen and your bowl will become flatter and shallower than when you cut it. It will be a bowl regardless of how you do it, so choose the procedure that feels best based on the piece of wood you have.

BOWL AND SAUCER

Fresh wood piece • knife
spoon gouge • sanding cloth • axe

DO IT THIS WAY

Cut the blank to the length you need and use the axe to rough out the outer shape of the bowl.

Draw the inner shape of the bowl and start digging out the bowl with the spoon gouge. Carve the edges in toward the center.

When you're happy with the inside, adjust the outside. Finish carving the bowl for the most part, but leave about 2 mm extra all around so that you have material left for fine shaping. If you plan to have a special edging or other detail that you want to be straight when the bowl is complete, save some extra wood so that you can even up the bowl again after it has dried. This applies primarily to the end grain in the bowl, which is most affected by the drying process.

Once the bowl has dried, start by flattening the underside of the bowl. Cut the worst off with the knife and finish it off with the sanding cloth.

When the bottom of the bowl is flat, straighten the upper edge, using the same trick as for the shrink box (Step 10 on page 104).

Finely carve and adjust the shape of the bowl inside.

After that, finely carve the bowl on the outside and treat the surface with your favorite oil.

Combs and hair clips

Does your hair stand straight up with static electricity every time you comb your hair? Avoid the frizzies with a handmade wooden comb, which is also softer than steel and plastic combs. And when your tresses are untangled, you can put your hair up in a carved hair barette.

Combs are carved with dry wood, and it is smart not to use stringy wood like oak, ash or elm because those types of wood can easily get break off into porous fibers. It is also good if the blank has as many annual rings as possible, that is, a piece of wood taken from the part of the tree that's as close to the bark as possible. Last but not least, it is important that the blank is straight and knot-free so that the teeth of the comb have maximum strength. If the fibers do not go all the way to the end of each tooth of the comb, it will be weak and there is a risk that the teeth will break when you're carving, not to mention when matted hair or a beard is being combed. Also, think about how you want your comb to look before you begin.

~~~~~~

COMB

**Dry wood piece • knife • axe • fine-toothed saw
sandpaper • clamp**

~~~~~~

DO IT THIS WAY

Comb › Cleave out a blank that is about 20 cm long and as wide as you want your comb to be. In order to keep the comb from breaking in the middle, make the spine quite thick, about 1 cm. Your comb will likely not be longer than 5–6 cm when it is complete, but a few extra centimeters are helpful to have when you clamp the blank to saw out the teeth. If your blank is fresh, add a few extra centimeters to the thickness, too (blanks with horizontal annual rings usually warp a lot when they dry).

When you make a comb, it is easiest to work with dry wood, so at this point if your blank is fresh, let it dry before continuing.

With the help of the axe and knife, thin down the blank on the side where the teeth will be sawed, 2–3 mm at the tip of the teeth and about 5–6 mm at the base are appropriate. Draw a line with a pencil so you know how deep you are going to saw the comb's teeth.

Clamp the wood piece vertically or horizontally, depending on what suits you. Vertical is easiest but clamping it horizontally to the kitchen table also works. Saw out your teeth from one end and work your way to the other end using a fine-toothed Japanese saw. Draw out

and saw one tooth at a time; if you saw a tooth here and a tooth there, there is a risk that there will be uneven spacing between the teeth.

Tip! If you want to clamp the subject vertically but do not have a workbench, you can remove the top drawer in a chest of drawers and then tighten the blank with a clamp against the side of the chest. If the top of the chest stands out over the sides, you may need to place a book between the chest and the blank so that it comes up over the edge. It's wise to put something between the blank and the piece of furniture to avoid scratches.

When you are finished sawing, cut the blank down to the size you want your comb to be.

Finish shaping the teeth with the knife. The easiest way to do this is to put the comb on a cutting board and carve against it so you won't damage any surfaces.

When your teeth are ready, shape them where they join to the back of the comb. Bevel both the tips of the teeth and the spine so the comb is comfortable for both scalp and hand.

Finally, fold a fine sandpaper, at least 180 grit, in half and draw it a few times between each tooth so that the grooves at the base of the teeth are rounded and gentler on the hair (or beard).

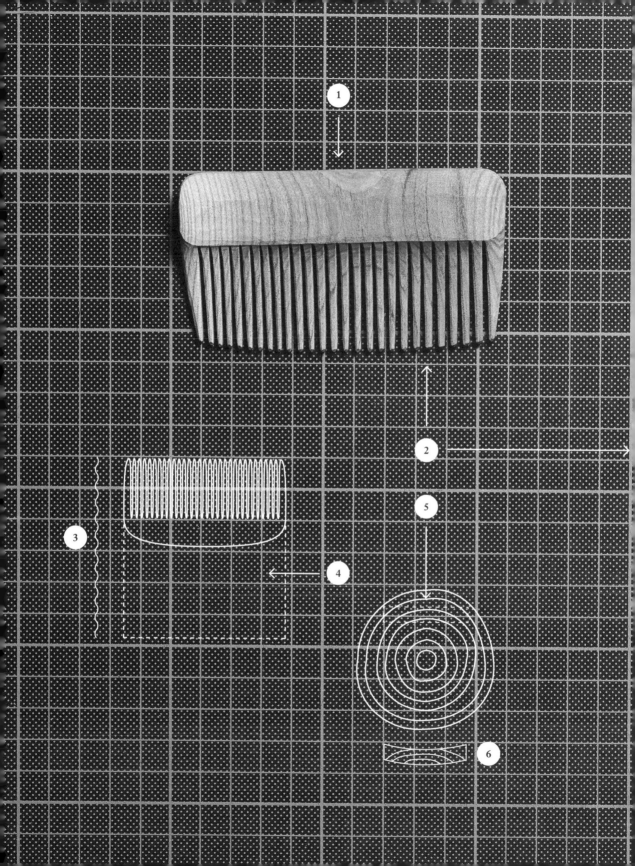

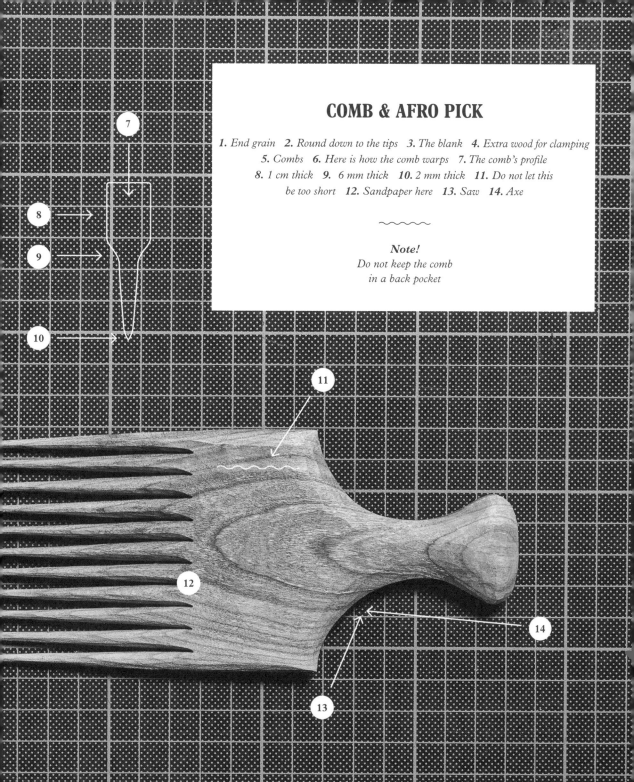

COMB & AFRO PICK

1. End grain   2. Round down to the tips   3. The blank   4. Extra wood for clamping
5. Combs   6. Here is how the comb warps   7. The comb's profile
8. 1 cm thick   9. 6 mm thick   10. 2 mm thick   11. Do not let this
be too short   12. Sandpaper here   13. Saw   14. Axe

~~~~~~~

Note!
Do not keep the comb
in a back pocket

AFRO PICK

Dry or fresh wood piece • knife
fine-toothed saw • sandpaper • clamp

~~~~~~~~~~

DO IT THIS WAY

Afro pick › Plan how your comb will look and even draw up a sketch to make the creation process easier.

Cleave out a blank that is approximately 1 cm thick and as long and as wide as you want it to be. As with the first comb, a blank with horizontal annual rings is preferable. Afro picks do not need as much finesse with the saw, so you can do several steps in fresh wood. It's worth noting, however, that the comb is likely to curve somewhat in the width while it dries. If you want to even it up again, include extra wood in the thickness when cutting out the blank.

Axe and carve out the outer form of the comb. Thin out on both sides the part where the teeth will be so that it goes from approximately 1 cm at the base to 3–4 mm at the teeth's end.

Draw the teeth. Clamp the blank with the side you plan to put the comb's handle on against the table or workbench, or whichever way you can. Saw out the teeth of the comb.

When sawing out the teeth, you can use 2 different methods: (1) Saw a cut between two teeth and carve out the wood up to the lines with the knife (carve from the saw cut's bottom out toward the tip of the teeth, otherwise the teeth break off), or (2) saw two cuts and pull out the wood in between. If your blank is fresh, let it dry when you have come this far.

Finely carve the teeth and finish carving the handle.

Finish off by folding a piece of fine sandpaper in half and draw it a few times against the tips of the teeth so that the comb is not so rough on the hair.

X

HAIR CLIPS

Fresh wood piece • drill • knife
spoon gouge • saw • axe

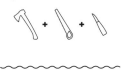

DO IT THIS WAY

Hair clip with pin › Cleave out a blank that has as many horizontal annual rings as possible, so it will be as strong as possible.

The end grain is turned vertically and the oval hole is across. The end grain above and below the hole are the weakest points of the clip, so make it a bit thicker in the middle and thinned out along the edges. You'll make the size of the hole according to the thickness of the hair that the clip is intended for.

Cleave out a blank that is about 2 cm thick and wide enough to accommodate the clip you plan to make. Cut it to the right length with the saw.

Take out another blank to make the pin for the hair clip, which should be about 1 cm thick and a few inches longer than the width of the clip. Narrow it down

slightly with the knife before leaving it to dry for later work.

Draw the shape of the clip onto the first blank and rough it out with the axe. It's best if you make the clip slightly curved so it fits the shape of the head. The outer shape can be done with the axe, but the inner shape is done with the knife. Let the finest side be the outside of the clip, but think about how the wood piece will warp as it dries.

Sketch out a hole onto the blank, and drill a hole in the middle of it. Choose a drill that is big enough for the knife blade to fit into the hole. Carve the hole to the desired size and shape.

Wooden pieces with horizontal annual rings can change a lot during the drying process. It may be wise not to carve too much on the clip before it has dried so that the end result will be as you imagined it.

When the hair clip has dried, finish shaping it and carve a nice surface. If you're going to make the hole bigger, it would be better for the durability of the clip to widen it horizontally rather than vertically.

Carve out the pin that will hold the hair and clip in place, and treat its surface with oil.

Bartender kit

Bartenders today chop their own ice and make tonic from scratch – so we thought it was time to reward these dedicated cocktail craftsmen with a set of carved bar tools. Of course, they also work well for us home bartenders who mostly just mix alcoholic soft drinks.

CITRUS JUICER

Fresh wood piece • knife
tape measure • saw • axe

DO IT THIS WAY

Citrus juicer › Cleave out a blank of about 15 × 5 × 5 cm. Draw the contours of the citrus juicer, on to the blank, then saw down to the stop cut and break out the handle. Shape the citrus juicer's head with the axe first and then with the knife. The shape should be mildly curved but end in a tip. The ridges will come later.

Smooth out the transition between the handle and the head and then continue to fix up the handle. When the shape of the citrus juicer looks nice and symmetrical, then it is time to carve the ridges.

Begin by measuring the circumference at the base of the head with a tape measure – it should be about 15 cm if you started from a 5 × 5 cm blank. Then ask yourself whether you can manage to cut 8 or 12 ridges. Depending on what you decide, divide the circumference by 8 or 12.

Using that number for the spacing interval between ridges, make small marks for each ridge onto the head. Draw lines from each mark you made up to the tip; these lines will be the tops of your ridges. It may be easier to draw with ink on fresh wood instead of with pencil.

Using the Japanese saw, saw a cut that's approximate 5 mm deep and that's exacly in between each line you have drawn for the ridges. The cut should end a few centimeters from the tip. Repeat the procedure between every line all the way around.

Take off a little bit of wood at a time with the knife until you have an angle from the line down to the bottom of the saw cut. Repeat this all the way around the head of the juicer. If you like, cut out the slices all the way to the tip, but it is unnecessary to put too much time on it before the blank has dried.

Let the blank dry, then shape it and carve a nice surface. When you carve the grooves into the citrus juicer's head, carefully cut from both sides and try to get the cuts to meet at the bottom. Make the grooves gradually shallower until they are only one millimeter deep at the tip. Surface treat with oil.

Muddler >To get extra flavor from fruits, herbs and spices, the bartender usually mashes them with a muddler. Often, muddling is done directly in the glass in which the drink will be served. Remember that the muddler should reach the bottom of the glass, so don't make it too big – 4 cm or less in diameter, to be on the safe side. A glass is usually not quite flat on the bottom, so to be able to crush it all, it is best to make the head slightly rounded so the muddler can make proper contact with the bottom of the glass.

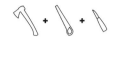
DO IT THIS WAY

Break out a blank about 25 × 4 × 4 cm. Draw the shape onto the blank, saw down the stop cut, and break out the handle. Shape the head of the muddler; first roughly with the axe and then smooth it out with the knife.

Even out the transition between the handle and head of the muddler, then continue to fix up the handle. When the muddler starts to look as you planned, let the blank dry for a week before proceeding.

Finish shaping the muddler and carve a nice surface. The top part is beveled or rounded off so that it is not so sharp when you touch it. The underside is made slightly rounded.

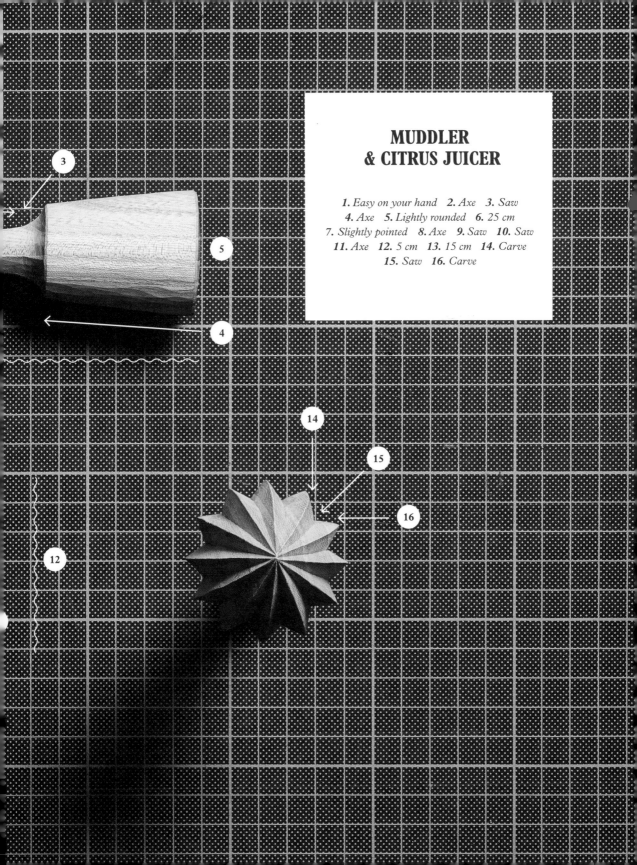

MUDDLER
& CITRUS JUICER

1. Easy on your hand   *2.* Axe   *3.* Saw
4. Axe   *5.* Lightly rounded   *6.* 25 cm
7. *Slightly pointed*   *8.* Axe   *9.* Saw   *10.* Saw
11. Axe   *12.* 5 cm   *13.* 15 cm   *14.* Carve
15. Saw   *16.* Carve

Bar spoon > To be able to stir in a tall glass, you need a spoon with an extra long handle. Follow the instructions for a spoon on page 78, but lengthen the handle by a few decimeters. A bar spoon is usually about 30 cm long.

Measuring jigger > The jigger measuring cup is made of end grain. The procedure is the same as for the espresso cup on page 93, but you're essentially making two espresso cups that are attached at the bottom. Be sure to save some extra wood to cut out a snazzy spout.

Bottle cork > A bottle cork is a finely shaped knob with a cork at the end. Instructions on how to make a knob can be found on page 112. After you have formed the knob, finish the cork by following these instructions.

BOTTLE CORK

**Dry wood piece • drill • knife
cork • saw
two-part epoxy • axe**

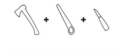

DO IT THIS WAY

Corks of different sizes and types can be purchased at home-brewing supply stores. Buy one of the models with a plastic head and remove the cap. Glue adheres badly or not at all to end grain, so in order for the cork to sit firmly in the knob you need to attach with a peg. Drill holes in the knob and cork with a 6 mm drill. Carve a dry wood peg that fits into the holes, cut it to the right length and glue it in place with wood glue. If you have a drill bit with the same diameter as the cork you can drill a 2–3 mm deep recess for the cork, which will make the knob and cork adhere even better.

STRAINER

Fresh wood piece • drill • knife
spoon gouge • saw • axe

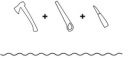

COCKTAIL STICK

Fresh wood piece • knife • axe

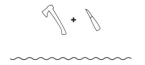

DO IT THIS WAY

Strainer › A bartender's strainer is basically a ladle with holes and a front lip. Drill the holes before cutting out the handle.

Begin by using the axe to roughly shape the bowl of the strainer, but wait to round the bowl underneath. Draw the outer and inner shapes of the bowl and where the holes should be, and do not forget to draw the front of the lip.

Drilling straight is easier said than done. An old trick to get straight holes is to drill in front of a mirror. In the mirror, you can make sure that you are not holding the drill at an angle. When the angle is correct from both sides and above, drill through the blank. Use a drill bit that is approximately 3 mm in diameter. When you have drilled the holes, round off the underside of the bowl and continue according to the instructions for the ladle on page 78.

DO IT THIS WAY

Cocktail stick › Making a stick to stir drinks does not have to be tricky. As long as the stick reaches above the rim and does not take up too much space in the glass, you have been successful. If you want a knob on your cocktail stick, you should start out from a thicker blank and then thin it down with the knife. Otherwise, you cleave out as thin a blank as you can and finely carve it with the knife.

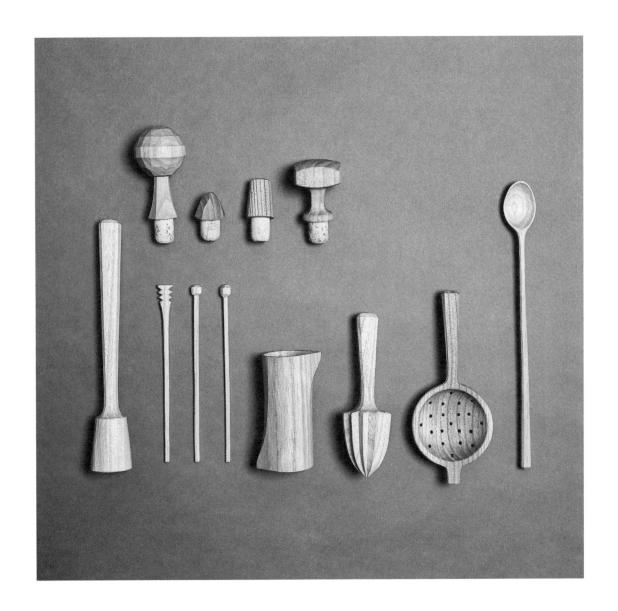

Rhythm instruments

Both adults and children can have great fun with these simple but nice-sounding rhythm instruments. Along with weapons for hunting, musical instruments are known to be some of the first objects that people learned to craft – archaeologists have found eight thousand-year-old drums, and the oldest instrument discovered is a flute made of bone that's thirty-five thousand years old.

~~~~~~

TAMBOURINE

Fresh forked branch • drill bottle caps • knife • saw • thick wire wood glue • pliers • hammer

~~~~~~

DO IT THIS WAY

Tambourine > To make a tambourine, you will need a branch fork. A piece of wood that is a fork where two branches meet – ideally one that is slightly larger than what you're planning your tambourine to be. A slightly larger branch can also be cleaved down to the desired size. The most important thing is that the branch fork has a shape that fits the purpose. Cut the blank so that all ends are about 5 cm longer than they will be when the tambourine is completed.

Rough out the form with knife and axe. If your blank already looks like the right size and shape, just peel off the bark.

Let the blank dry for a couple of days so the wood will be hard and you can get a sharp cut and smooth surface when carving the final shape.

Once the blank has dried, you will most likely find that it has split at the ends. The cracks usually do not spread far into the wood piece, so when you saw off the extra centimeters you saved, you will have also removed the cracks.

Carving a branch fork is easier said than done. In the crook where the two branches join, the fibers can cross and change direction several times within just a few centimeters. With such conditions, it may best to carve horizontally rather than vertically. Carving the width usually also works well if you have a bump or knot in the blank. Once you have finished carving the branch fork, it is time to treat it with oil.

$\longrightarrow\longrightarrow$

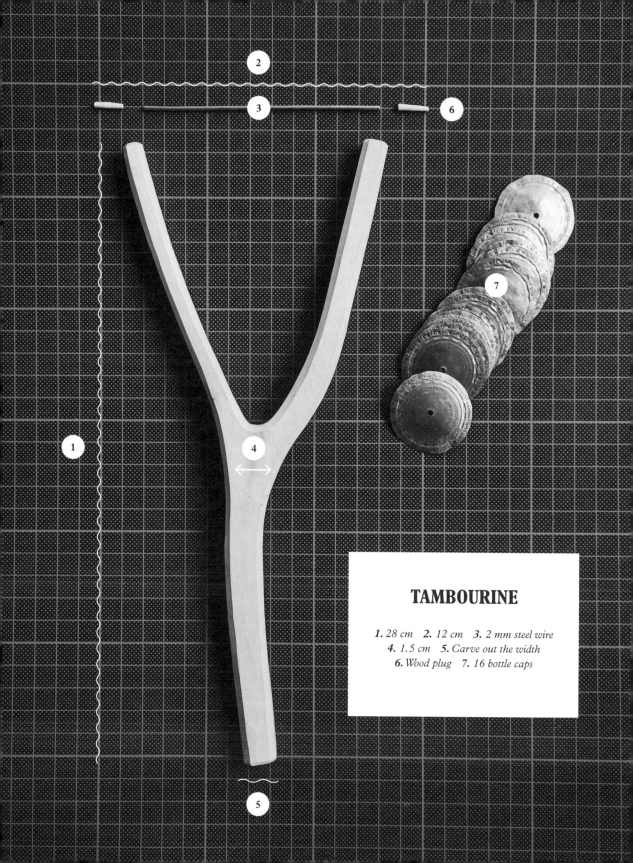

TAMBOURINE

1. 28 cm   *2.* 12 cm   *3.* 2 mm steel wire
4. 1.5 cm   *5.* Carve out the width
6. Wood plug   *7.* 16 bottle caps

Flattened bottle caps become more like cymbals and also rattle a little more. Begin by bending out the edges of the caps a bit with pliers. When that is done, flatten out the caps with a hammer; the chopping block works well as a base underneath if you do not have an anvil. Finish by drilling a hole in the center of the caps with a drill bit that is one millimeter thicker than the steel wire onto which you are going to thread the caps. The easiest way is to thread the caps on a thick wire that is not easy to bend – 2–3 mm works well.

Drill holes straight through the branch fork with a drill bit that has the same thickness as the steel wire. Cut a piece of steel wire that is long enough to go from one hole to the other and has an extra 5–6 mm sticking out of the branch fork on both sides. Feed the steel wire through one hole, thread on the caps, and then stick the wire through the other hole using the pliers. Make sure that both ends of the steel wire are sticking out evenly on both sides. Finish by carving two plugs and gluing them into the holes so that the steel wire is sealed in and stays in place. Once the glue has dried you can cut off what is still sticking out of the plugs.

~~~~~~~~~~~~

MARACAS

**Dry wood piece • drill
metal or plastic container
knife • glue • axe**

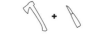

~~~~~~~~~~~~

DO IT THIS WAY

Maracas › Start with a nice can containing a liquid food item that will be easy to drain through a hole that's about 8 mm wide. Plain chicken broth and coconut milk come out without any problems, Stewed or diced tomatoes will take longer.

Mark the center point of the two ends of the can with a pen. Drilling in metal can be a little tricky. It is difficult for the drill to take hold, and often the hole does not end up where you intended. If you hit a neat stroke with a nail on the mark, the drill will get a better grip in the metal and the hole will end up where you want it.

Drill a hole at each end of the can with an 8 mm drill and empty the contents.

When you are going to make the handle, it is worth taking some extra time to find a straight and knot-free blank. In this case, there is no great advantage to working with fresh wood; with a good enough stick you can do the whole handle in one sweep.

Cut out a blank that is wide enough and a little longer than you're planning your handle to be.

Shape the blank with the ax to make it square. Saw off another piece and save it. This will be the knob that goes on top of the can.

Start by carving the "heel" and the part of the handle that will go through the can. Mark out where on the blank you want the can to sit and saw a cut with a fine-toothed saw along the line all the way around. Better to saw too shallow than too deep.

Gently break out the wood from the top down to the sawed cut with the axe. Gently tap the axe's neck with a wooden mallet or stick. This way, you can go more carefully and stop if the crack seems to go off somewhere you do not want.

When you have split off as much wood as you can with the axe, finish with the knife until you can pull the can onto the handle.

Shape the visible part of the handle.

Drill a hole in the piece of wood that will be your knob. The depth of the hole

you drill depends on how you planned the knob to look. However, at least 1 cm is recommended so that it stays firmly in place.

Shape the knob.

When the knob and handle are ready, it is time to treat the surface with oil. Be careful not to oil the parts that will be glued.

Fill the can with a fair amount of something like rice, lentils, pebbles or sand. The maracas sound different depending on what you put inside, so try it out until you get a sound you like.

Hold the maraca by the handle and glue on the knob. It might be good to clamp the knob and the handle when gluing so that the can is pressed between the parts.

If you want to glue the can to the handle, use a glue that's stronger than wood glue. Two-part epoxy adheres well on both wood and metal and is guaranteed to hold the can in place. Take care and wear protective gloves; epoxy glue is no fun to get on your skin and hands.

TIPS!

If you want to make it a little easier for yourself, make the handle in three parts: the heel, the top of the handle that goes into the can, and the knob. Make the top of the handle go 5–6 cm into the handle and put a little wood glue into the hole so that the parts fit together properly.

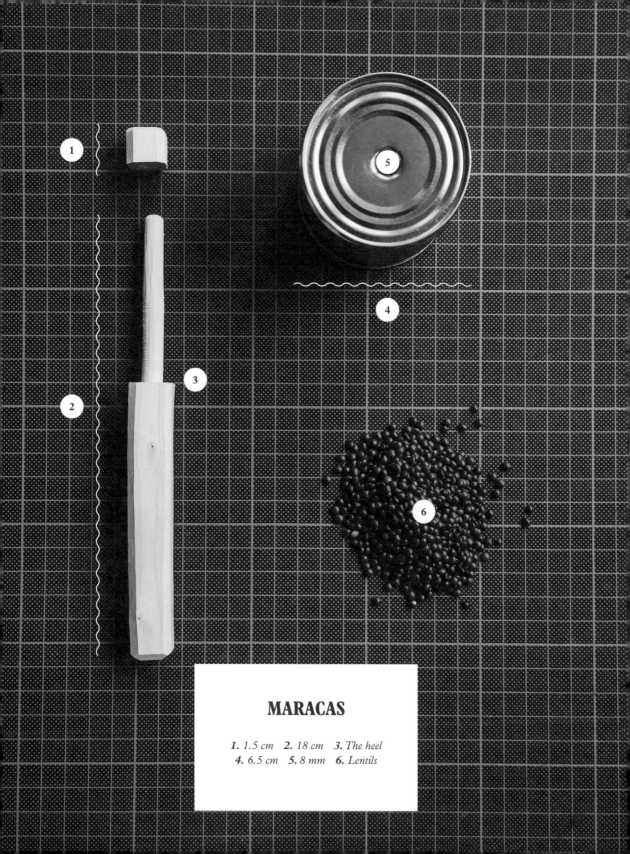

MARACAS

1. 1.5 cm   *2.* 18 cm   *3.* The heel
4. 6.5 cm   *5.* 8 mm   *6.* Lentils

GÜIRO

Fresh or dry wood piece • drill bit and drill machine • saw • knife• axe

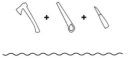

~~~~~~~~~~~~

DO IT THIS WAY

Güiro > Begin by looking for a straight and knot-free blank, preferably in a slightly harder wood – not pine.

Roughly shape the blank with an axe so the blank is approximately 25 × 5 × 5 cm.

Be sure to use both hands when drilling holes into the blank. This is especially true when drilling into fresh wood with a large drill. Sometimes it can be difficult for the drill to get a grip in fresh wood and you have to press and coax a bit with the drill so that it grips. You may need to hold fresh wood with both hands to prevent the risk of drilling nicks in it. If you do not have a workbench to clamp the blank to, use your imagination to clamp the piece onto something else so that you can use both hands. If nothing else, you can always tighten the clamp directly onto the blank and then stand on it while drilling down. Drill a hole between 6–9 cm deep.
Draw the shape you want your güiro to have. Use the hole you drilled as a guide and make sure the blank does not taper off too sharply toward the handle. Include some extra wood so that it is not too fragile. Shape with the axe. If your blank is fresh, let it dry before continuing.

Before you carve the grooves, it is best to start drawing lines in about 3–4 mm intervals; every other line marks a ridge and the other lines are the grooves in between. Using a fine-toothed saw, make a cut that is approximately 3 mm deep on a groove line. You can put a piece of tape on the saw blade at the same distance from the tip of the teeth as the cut should be deep. Carve gradually from both sides down to the bottom of the saw cut until you have formed a V. Begin at the top and work down toward the handle. Saw one cut at a time and carve one V at a time, then it does not matter if a V comes out a bit wider than another.

You will be surprised at the difference between the sound before and after you have sawed the güiro. The tone becomes deeper and the resonance is greater. Shape the güiro into the handle and saw a cut straight over the center of the handle and down until you are a few millimeters from the bottom of the handle. Use a coping saw or Japanese saw without a back. The most important thing is that the saw blade is fine-toothed and not too thick.

Last but not least, carve out a stick to play your güiro with. You get the best sound if it is narrow enough to go down between the grooves of the güiro.

Figures and folk caricatures

Sweden is famous for its carved wooden figures and skilled woodcarvers. Emil Janel, Axel "Döderhultaren" Petersson and Carl Johan Trygg and his sons are well-known and appreciated artists of their time. The most famous woodcarver of all is, however, an imaginary prankster who, in order to avoid his father's angry outbursts, would flee to the toolshed. There, he spent his time carving figures with a saw, axe and knife, as good a way to pass the time as any.

The Swedish model of wood carving is characterized by the use of very few tools. We pride ourselves on using only knives when we cut out folk caricatures and shapes, and we do not sand away the carved surface. At some time, every Swede must have carved figures in their summer cabins, given the large number of figures found at flea markets, secondhand stores, and antique stores around Sweden.

Outside Sweden, this style is usually called Scandinavian flat-plane wood carving. Elsewhere in the world, small wood sculptures are usually carved using small gouges or sculpting chisels, and then they are typically sanded.

Carving a fish is a good first challenge. The basic shape is relatively simple and it is easy to find a suitable blank. Emil Janel and Döderhultaren liked to work with alder, the Trygg family carved their figures out of linden; the figures in this book are made of birch. The type of wood you prefer to carve with is a matter of taste. It's best to start with a relatively dry piece of wood. A blank that has been cleaved up for a while works very well. If you saw off the cracks with a little margin, you can be relatively certain that no new cracks will occur.

FISH

Dry or fresh wood piece
knife • saw • axe

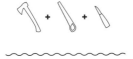

DO IT THIS WAY

Fish › 1. If you're a beginner, it's wise to start by sketching how you want the figure to look. If you're carving a fish, drawing just the profile is enough. If you make an old man, it is a good idea to draw it from at least two perspectives. When the sketch is complete, use the axe to cut out a blank for your figure. Cut the sides till they're somewhat smooth and draw the figure.

2. Roughly cut out the shape. You can do a lot with a saw and axe, and with a coping saw, you can saw a piece in a few minutes that would have taken hours to carve away. Using the saw, remove as much wood as you can before starting in with the knife. Carving away a lot of wood takes a toll on the knife, hands and patience.

3. Carve with the knife and re-draw the lines that disappeared during rough cutting.

4. Begin to round off or bevel out shapes and differences in depth. Wait to fine-tune and carve details until the whole form is correct. Sometimes what you have carved can look good from one angle but not so good from another, and you may need to correct it. It would be a shame to carve away something you took time to get right. When carving a difference in depths, start by making a cut down with the tip of the knife, then carve down. Sometimes, it is a good idea to support the blank against something when making the cuts so you can push down on the knife using the hand that's not already holding it. Often, you have to cut down and carve away a couple of times before reaching the right depth.

5. When the figure looks good proportionally and you have carved out the dimensions, you can start carving the details and making it look nice. It is best to have a really sharp knife with a long tip to carve into the tight spaces and get a good cut. Adjust your grip as needed. When carving small details, you do not need to use much strength. Hold the knife like a pencil with your fingers away from the blade and push a little with your other hand. You can also carve toward your thumb with your fingers far ahead of the blade. For extra control, you can press on the back of the blade with the hand that is holding the blank. In this way, you can carve slowly and with great control.